Blockchainopoly

How Blockchain Changes the Rules of the Game

Steve Hoberman

Technics Publications

Published by:

2 Lindsley Road, Basking Ridge, NJ 07920 USA
https://www.TechnicsPub.com

Edited by Lauren McCafferty and Sadie Hoberman
Cover design by Lorena Molinari
Cartoons by Mateusz Wieczorek

First Printing 2018
Copyright © 2018 by Steve Hoberman

ISBN, print ed.	9781634621724
ISBN, Kindle ed.	9781634623452
ISBN, ePub ed.	9781634623469
ISBN, Audio ed.	9781634621892

Library of Congress Control Number: 2018902017

Contents

Introduction _____ 1

PART 1: About Blockchain_____ **9**

Chapter 1: Explanation_____ 13

Part II: Blockchain Usage _____ **43**

Chapter 2: Blockchain within Finance_____ 55

Chapter 3: Blockchain within Insurance _____ 65

Chapter 4: Blockchain within Government _____ 75

Chapter 5: Blockchain within Manufacturing and Retail___ 85

Chapter 6: Blockchain within Utilities _____ 95

Chapter 7: Blockchain within Healthcare _____ 103

Chapter 8: Blockchain within Nonprofit _____ 111

Chapter 9: Blockchain within Media _____ 119

Part III: Blockchain Impact _____ **129**

Chapter 10: Data Governance _____ 133

Chapter 11: Data Architecture_____ 141

Chapter 12: Data Modeling and Design_____ 149

Chapter 13: Data Storage and Operations_____ 159

Chapter 14: Data Security _____ 165

Chapter 15: Data Integration and Interoperability _____ 171

Chapter 16: Document and Content Management _____ 179

Chapter 17: Reference and Master Data _____ 185

Chapter 18: Data Warehousing and Business Intelligence_ 191

Chapter 19: Metadata Management_____ 199

Chapter 20: Data Quality _____ 205

Conclusion _____ 211

Index _____ 217

Introduction

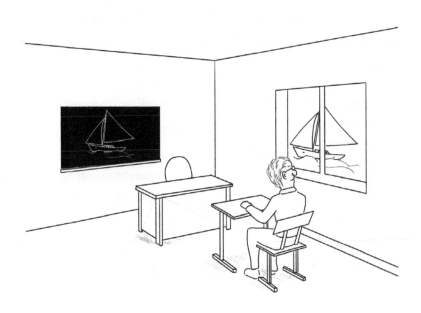

I was a computer science major in college. I won't tell you my age, but I will say the hot programming language at the time was Pascal. If you knew Pascal, you could demand top dollar when you graduated. This made my computer science friends and me impatient and eager to learn this new technology.

As you can imagine, then, we were disappointed when the first few semesters came and went without any mention of Pascal. The languages we were using were BASIC, Fortran, and yes, even Assembly. (Assembly was pure torture, by the way. It was the class where the first day the professor said, "Look to your right, look to your left, only one of you will be here by the end of the semester.")

Our professors emphasized programming concepts and principles, instead of learning the most popular new programming language. We spent lots of time on concepts including sequence; conditionals, such as IF-THEN statements; and iteratives, like WHILE loops. Our professors constantly stressed principles such as limiting procedures to one function, keeping code simple, indenting for readability, avoiding the dreaded GOTO statement, and testing and retesting.

When they finally taught Pascal in senior year, my friends and I were surprised by how quickly we picked up the language. It was so easy! In graduate school, I found the C programming language just as easy to master. Each time a shiny new programming language hit the marketplace, it was easy to learn because I knew the programming concepts and principles.

The moral of the story:

> Avoid getting hypnotized by the job recruiter's gold pocket watch. Ignore the songs from the vendor's sirens. Do not walk into the light. Instead, learn the concepts and principles first, and then afterwards figure out how the new technology delivers.

We can apply this principle of learning the concepts before the technology to just about anything. A few years ago, I took sailing lessons. I just wanted to get the boat out in the water and start sailing, but my instructor spent hours in a classroom (without air conditioning) describing how to leverage the wind. For instance, one of his favorite concepts was picturing a clock, where the wind is at 12:00 and the bow of the sailboat is directed at a certain digit on the clock. We listened to him lecture for hours, using magnets on a whiteboard to represent the position of the sailboat with respect to the wind. We needed to understand the concept of wind before deploying the technology of the sailboat.

Sailing two months a year in New Jersey will never make me a great sailor, but I have become a skilled data modeler modeling data 12 months a year for the last 30 years.

A data modeler applies core concepts and principles to building databases. Just like in programming languages and sailing, the concepts and principles required for good database design must be mastered before deploying the technology of the database.

The data modeling process often starts off with talking to business professionals about their application requirements. Doing this can help the modeler understand project scope, and can clarify the meanings of core concepts such as customer, product, and account. Furthermore, good design principles must be followed; these include grouping similar properties together, planning for unknown requirements, and removing data redundancy.

The end result of all this data modeling work is a precise visual called the "data model." It is described as "precise" because there is exactly one way to read a data model. Take this data model for example:

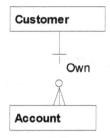

This model can be read exactly one way:

- Each Customer may own one or many Accounts.
- Each Account must be owned by one Customer.

This means, for example, that Bob can own Accounts 125 and 789. Each of those two accounts must be owned by one and only one customer such as Bob.

These precise diagrams solve many communication issues that could arise during development. The data model becomes a powerful communication tool for understanding the data, and is often used in building, supporting, and integrating software systems.

In short, data modelers are trained to transform ambiguity into precision. If you're interested in learning more about data modeling, start with my book *Data Modeling Made Simple*.

We know that focusing first on the concepts and principles allows us to better leverage technology. Additionally, if these concepts and principles are conveyed to users very precisely, they will be more easily committed to memory. Therefore I—your trusted data modeler—will be your guide through the blockchain jungle. During your read, I will use my learned communication skills to illuminate the core concepts behind the world of blockchain.

This book will not teach you how to build a blockchain application. Instead, this book will teach you something much more valuable: the concepts and principles that provide the foundation for building any blockchain application.

This book comprises three parts:

1. **Explanation**. Part I will explain the principles underlying blockchain. A precise and concise definition is provided, distinguishing blockchain from blockchain architecture. Variations of blockchain are explored based upon the concepts of purpose and scope.

2. **Usage**. Now that you understand blockchain, where do you use it? The motivation behind building a blockchain application must include at least one of these five drivers: transparency, streamlining, privacy, permanence, or distribution. For each of these five drivers, we'll show examples of blockchain use in the sectors of finance, insurance, government, manufacturing, retail, utilities, healthcare, nonprofit, and media. Process diagrams will illustrate each usage through inputs, guides, enablers, and outputs. Also examined are the risks of applying these usages, such as cooperation, incentives, and change.

3. **Impact.** Now that you know where to use blockchain, how will it impact the existing IT (Information Technology) environment? Part III explores how blockchain will affect data management. The Data Management Body of Knowledge 2nd Edition (DAMA-DMBOK2) is an amazing book that defines the data management field along with the complex relationships that exist between the various data management disciplines, such as between data governance and data architecture. Learn how blockchain will impact each of the 11 data management disciplines within DAMA-DMBOK2.

This book is for those who need and want to learn about blockchain. Once you—as a business or IT professional—understand the concepts and principles, you can position yourself, department, and organization to benefit and leverage blockchain technology.

As you begin to understand the immense power and potential of blockchain, you'll come to recognize it as a truly disruptive technology—just like the wheel, printing press, computer, web, smartphone, or cloud. And just like these other groundbreaking technologies, once you understand the underlying principles and use them to build a solid foundation, the opportunities are endless.

PART 1

About Blockchain

I love the board game Monopoly®. With the roll of the dice, we work our way around the board, buying properties, building hotels, and conducting financial transactions with other players and with the bank.

The banker in Monopoly is a very powerful role. After all, the banker controls all of the money. Almost all of the financial transactions require the banker acting as intermediary.

We trust that the banker has our best interest in mind. We trust that he or she will give us the correct change in financial transactions and act with integrity and responsibility.

Sometimes however, the powerful banker violates our trust and leverages their power for ulterior motives. I have played quite a few rounds of Monopoly where money mysteriously vanishes from the bank and appears in the banker's own account. Sometimes the banker "forgets" to give me $200 for passing Go. Sometimes a friend of the banker magically emerges from near-bankruptcy with a stack of bills followed by laughter or winks between player and banker.

The Monopoly banker is powerful, and can be generalized as any central power authority in our business or personal lives. A central power authority could be considered any person or organization who has a monopoly on one or more processes, such as settling financial transactions, grading diamonds, registering intellectual property, or selling songs. In order to participate in a process, we often interact with a central power authority. Central power authorities are everywhere—in every aspect of our work and play, from business to government to leisure.

What if we could remove the central power authority from the process? Or, at a minimum, reduce the overarching influence of that central power authority? What if we could play the board game Monopoly without the banker? What if all of the Monopoly players could share the role of banker?

We will see in the following chapter that blockchain is all about sharing responsibility and removing the monopoly on the central power authority. Our goal here is to go from a monopoly to a "blockchainopoly."

A blockchainopoly creates shared responsibility in executing a process, as opposed to the powerful position of a central power authority. However, blockchainopoly does not always mean removing the powerful monopoly position completely from the process. Often the organization owning the monopoly still plays an important role in the blockchain application.

Blockchain changes the rules of the game.

CHAPTER 1

Explanation

This chapter will explain the principles underlying blockchain. A precise and concise definition is provided, distinguishing blockchain from blockchain architecture. Variations of blockchain are explored based upon the concepts of purpose and scope.

GAME CHANGERS EVERY DECADE

At this point, it goes without saying that major technologies regularly emerge that completely disrupt the tech environment. In fact, there has been at least one of these major "game changers" in every recent decade.

In the 1970s the mainframe was the game changer. This powerful computer allowed governments and large organizations to automate many tasks that were previously manual, and centralize, store, and access lots of data.

In the 1980s, it was the personal computer (PC) that rocked the tech world. The PC allowed both large and small organizations as well as households to automate many types of tasks and store and access much more data.

My first PC was the Commodore 64. 64 kilobytes of RAM—who would ever need more? I remember storing a set of instructions on a cassette for allowing a robot arm to move a penny from one pile to another. I felt as if I owned the most powerful computer in the world.

The technology game was changed yet again in the 1990s thanks to the web. Who would have thought that creating an intuitive graphical user interface over the Internet and virtualizing IP addresses into URLs would change the world? But it did. Now we can access data and services from computers all over the world.

Of course, at the turn of the century, we changed the game again by putting all of this into our pockets. Mobile computing ruled the 2000s as a disruptive force in technology. We could now access the services and data from computers all over the world anywhere we go.

Each of these technological "game changers" brings us closer to:

> Getting the **right** information to the **right** people at the **right** time.

However, all of these previous game changers have enabled central power authorities to control the processes for getting the right information to the right people at the right time. If I want to purchase 100 shares of IBM, the Depository Trust Company (DTC) will control the process. If I want to download a Paul Simon song, iTunes will control the process. If I want to copyright this book, a government intellectual property agency will control the process.

This is where blockchain emerges as the next big game changer. It revolutionizes the rules of the game because it allows us to "get the right information to the right people at the right time" using shared responsibility instead of the central power authority. In fact, blockchain changes our maxim to:

> *Getting the right information to the right people at the right time, without relying on a central power authority.*

BLOCKCHAIN IN THREE WORDS

Before we get much further, let's take a moment to clearly define just what blockchain is. At the most fundamental level, blockchain is an *immutable shared ledger*. Let's look more closely at the terms *ledger*, *shared*, and *immutable*.

LEDGER

Blockchain is a *ledger*. A ledger is a fancy word for a spreadsheet. The simplest form of a spreadsheet is a T-account, a two-column spreadsheet that maintains a list of credits and debits. For example, if I buy a new computer for $500, this could be both a debit to my assets and a credit to my liabilities:

	Asset
Debit	Credit
$500	

	Liability
Debit	Credit
	$500

A ledger can be any spreadsheet, simple or complex. A ledger can store the details of transactions, such as stock trades, insurance claims, or product orders. A ledger can store a list of inventory or assets owned by an individual or company. A ledger can even store a record of our life's events, such as when we graduated high school, got married, or retired.

We can generalize a ledger to be any organized set of information. The information in a spreadsheet is described as "organized" because it is grouped into sets by column headings.

Blockchain ledgers are revolutionary because the data is not just organized into sets, but also captured by chronology, with each new row in the spreadsheet forever linked to the previous row.

SHARED LEDGER

Blockchain is a *shared* ledger. Instead of a business or government agency managing the process of making changes to or accessing the ledger, the responsibility is "shared." Shared means the central power authority is replaced by multiple computers. Each computer maintains a copy of the ledger, and is often called a "recordkeeper."

In the following figure, each cube represents a ledger; each disc underneath represents a computer playing the role of recordkeeper.

The recordkeepers communicate with each other to ensure that their ledgers remain current and accurate.

The relatively simple act of sharing blockchain ledgers is truly game changing, because it removes or minimizes the need for a central power authority, and instead allows the information to be recorded by chronology by multiple computers.

IMMUTABLE SHARED LEDGER

Blockchain is an *immutable* shared ledger. If you work in Information Technology (IT), you might be familiar with the acronym CRUD, which stands for Create, Read, Update, and Delete. CRUD means that within an application, data can be created and stored, read and used, updated, and eventually deleted.

In blockchain, we can only do the first two: Create and Read. We can never Update or Delete data once it has been saved to the ledger. The ledger exists to write and read only. Immutable means data cannot be changed; we cannot edit history. Once I purchased that computer for $500, that price can never be updated to $400 or $600.

Making shared ledgers immutable has been a game changer in terms of accountability and transparency. All of the information that has been written to the ledger is kept up-to-date and accurate by the recordkeepers, and provides a permanent history of events transpired— without concerns that someone can tamper with the data.

BLOCKCHAIN ARCHITECTURE

I would like to give my brother $10 for his birthday. Okay, so I am not a generous brother, but it's the thought that counts. There are a number of ways I can give the $10 gift:

- I can give it to him when I see him in person

- I can mail it to his address

- I can do a bank transfer from my account to his

- I can send through a service such as Western Union or PayPal

- I can send using a digital currency such as Bitcoin

If I give him the $10 in person or mail it to him, there most likely is no record that I have given such a generous gift. He might give me only $5 for my birthday, and there would be no proof that I gave him $10.

The bank transfers and services such as Western Union will provide a record of the transaction, but there are often hefty fees involved.

Let's go for the digital currency option. Bitcoin is the first application to be built using blockchain. Bitcoin is one of many digital currency transfer applications. (We will revisit the word "application" shortly.) The transaction might be recorded in the Bitcoin blockchain ledger as:

Steve	Gary
-$10	$10

This is just a single ledger, though. Blockchain requires multiple ledgers, each maintained by a recordkeeper. For this example, let's say there are three ledgers and therefore three recordkeepers:

Recordkeeper A	
Steve	Gary
-$10	$10

Recordkeeper B	
Steve	Gary
-$10	$10

Recordkeeper C	
Steve	Gary
-$10	$10

There are two questions at this point:

1. I don't want the world to know that I, Steve, just gave my brother Gary $10. In addition to not letting the world know that I am a cheap brother, there's also a privacy issue. How do I conduct this financial transaction anonymously?

2. There are three spreadsheets. How does the $10 transfer get recorded in all three? If I maintained these three spreadsheets manually, I could make the change to all three—I would likely make a mistake in one or more. And in the real world,

maybe the "mistakes" could be intentional, like that Monopoly banker "forgetting" to give me $200 for passing Go. How do we ensure integrity in the system?

Let's explore both questions.

HOW DO WE CONDUCT BUSINESS ANONYMOUSLY?

We wear masks when we conduct business on blockchain. For example, to protect my identity and my brother's identity, I may wear a Darth Vader mask and my brother a Yoda mask:

Recordkeeper A	
Darth	Yoda
-$10	$10

Recordkeeper B	
Darth	Yoda
-$10	$10

Recordkeeper C	
Darth	Yoda
-$10	$10

This system works fine until someone else puts on a Yoda mask, and that $10 accidently goes to some stranger in Des Moines instead of to my brother.

This is where identifiers are useful. If there is a unique ID for me and one for my brother, and I know his unique ID, I can make the transfer knowing that it will go to him, and he will know that it comes from me. So if my unique ID is 123 and his is 789, our transaction would look like this:

Recordkeeper A	
123	789
-$10	$10

Recordkeeper B	
123	789
-$10	$10

Recordkeeper C	
123	789
-$10	$10

The 123 and 789 are called "public keys" in blockchain. A public key is a unique identifier assigned to users of a blockchain application. "Public" means that anyone in the world can see it. The public keys identify the users in the blockchain ledger.

Public keys allow us to participate in processes anonymously, without exposing identifiers that have intrinsic value, such as credit card numbers or social security numbers.

How does the system know that 123 is me and 789 is my brother if our public keys do not contain any identifying information to tie them to us?

The actual, identifying keys are called "private keys" in blockchain. I know my private key, which has intrinsic value similar to a social security number, and my brother knows his private key.

Private keys are never exposed on blockchain. If someone learned someone else's private key, they could perform any number of actions or initiate any transactions from this private key, which could lead to loss of money or identity. Private keys are often kept safe in special obscuring software called "wallets."

We use our public key to conduct transactions, and the recordkeepers confirm the mapping back to our private key. A public key is created from a private key using a secret code. The technical name for this process is called asymmetric-key cryptography.[1]

As an additional layer of security, we often create "addresses" based upon our public keys. It would be difficult to crack the code to identify a private key from a public key. It would be next to impossible to crack the code to identify a public key from an address, and *then* the private key from the public key.

An address is created from a public key using a process called "hashing." Hashing means creating a fixed-length code based upon some digital data. This code is called a "hash," and is created with a complex formula that cannot easily be hacked. A hash is deterministic, meaning that the same input data will always produce the same hash.

A hash is a digital fingerprint of some digital data. Hashing is used in blockchain for obscuring not just public keys, but also for obscuring transactions and assets. If you would like to play with hashing, visit http://bit.ly/2HEHoR8.

There is a number of hash algorithms used in blockchain applications. One very common one is the Secure Hash Algorithm (SHA), which generates a 64-character code based upon any document or transaction or public key.

---

[1] FIPS Publication 186-4, Digital Signature Standard specifies a common algorithm for digital signing used in blockchain technologies: Elliptic Curve Digital Signature Algorithm (ECDSA).

Regardless of the size of the content being hashed, the hash code will always be a fixed length, such as 64 characters in the case of SHA. These long character codes become addresses in blockchain, and represent the digital fingerprints for the actual information being disguised.

The early adopters of blockchain quickly realized the importance of a complex hash, and adopted a very secure one. Blockchain's hash algorithm is so tough that it requires very powerful computers to map an address back to a public key.

A person can own many private keys, and each private key is associated with one public key, and each public key may be associated with one or more addresses. Public keys are typically too long to memorize, so they are often copied and pasted, or associated with a QR code.

HOW DO WE ENSURE INTEGRITY IN THE SYSTEM?

Now let's return to our second concern about my very generous birthday gift to my brother. What if there is a data quality issue in the spreadsheets? I might have genuinely mistyped the financial amount, or maybe it's that Monopoly banker again, trying to fudge numbers to make sure he or she wins the game. So how can we trust the system?

To understand how blockchain ensures integrity in the system, come back with me in time a couple of thousand years. There is a walled city in China besieged by a large army divided into ten groups, each controlled by a general.

The generals communicate with each through messengers on horseback. No smartphones.

If a majority of the generals attack with their men, they can defeat the city. However, if only one or two armies attack, there will be certain defeat.

The generals vote to decide whether to attack or not. If a majority votes to attack, they all attack and will most likely win. Even if six generals attack, they will win—as long as it is a majority.

The problem, though, is that the generals don't trust each other. There are rumors about who is a traitor and who is loyal. So a general can send a soldier on horseback to a neighboring general communicating an attack, yet only that general has been given the signal. The general and his men might then attack, and being the only army that attacks, there is certain defeat for this one army.

So nobody knows for sure who is loyal and who is a traitor. How can they coordinate an attack if no one is to be trusted?

This classic challenge is called the Byzantine Generals' Problem.

One solution to this challenge is to create a puzzle, also known as a cryptograph. Only those generals who are loyal would be able to solve it. As long as a majority of generals can successfully solve the puzzle, there will be a favorable outcome for the army.

The recordkeepers in blockchain are like the generals. A transaction which has been hashed becomes the puzzle to solve.

To solve the puzzle, the recordkeepers must "unhash" the hash; sometimes solving only part of the hash is sufficient.

The recordkeepers often work independently to "unhash" the hash, to solve the puzzle and confirm that a transaction is valid. For any given transaction, part of the hash coding involves the previously accepted block in blockchain. This allows blocks to be linked together into a "chain." Hence the name "blockchain." All hashes contain the most recently accepted block in blockchain, except for the first block, which is called the "genesis block."

Media outlet CoinDesk explained this linking concept as follows: "Because each block's hash is produced using the hash of the block before it, it becomes a digital version of a wax seal. It confirms that this block — and every block after it — is legitimate, because if you tampered with it, everyone would know."[2]

The first recordkeeper that successfully solves the hash wins. There is often an incentive for winning, such as

---

[2] http://bit.ly/2E0hiKj.

financial compensation. This recordkeeper then shares their solution with the other recordkeepers, who check the winning recordkeeper's work. It is much easier to double-check a solved hash than to solve it from the beginning. As long as a certain percentage of recordkeepers are able to either solve or confirm the solution to the hash (usually a majority), the transaction is "validated" and recorded on the blockchain. This process of confirming the validity of a transaction is called "proof of work."

Each validated transaction is added to a block in the blockchain. A block in blockchain can contain multiple transactions.

The recordkeepers create these puzzles and solve them by communicating with each other over a network, just like the generals using horses. The language the recordkeepers use over the network is called a "protocol." The protocol allows the recordkeepers to communicate with each other, as the recordkeepers must work together to validate transactions.

There could be several, dozens, hundreds, or thousands of recordkeepers. The number of recordkeepers depends on many factors including security and performance. Performance in this context refers to the number of transactions that can be processed in a certain amount of time. For example, if 20 recordkeepers are needed to validate a transaction instead of 50 recordkeepers, each transaction can be completed faster taking less time, but the risk of a fraudulent transaction is greater (since fewer recordkeepers are monitoring it).

The protocol is also used to execute contracts. Executing contracts means running programming code when certain conditions are true. In other words, IF a certain condition becomes true, THEN execute code to do something (for instance, initiate a transaction). Such IF-THEN statements are common programming constructs, and are used frequently in blockchain applications. We will talk more about contracts and IF-THEN statements shortly.

The protocol is built on top of the ledgers. We can imagine something like this:

Protocol		
Recordkeeper A	Recordkeeper B	Recordkeeper C
Ledger	Ledger	Ledger

There are two levels here: the protocol and the ledger. Each level is also called a "tier." The ledger is also known as the data tier, and the protocol tier is also known as the function tier.

This two-tiered environment allows for trusted communication among the recordkeepers and for the execution of contracts. Examples of different blockchain protocols include Bitcoin, Ripple, and Ethereum.

There is one more tier on top of the protocol, which is the application that automates the process. The blockchain architecture contains three tiers. "Blockchain" refers to the ledger (which is the first tier), and "Blockchain architecture" includes the application, protocol, and ledger.

The application tier automates one or more business processes and enhances a user experience. A blockchain application would appear to the user as any other typical application. That is, the application hides the protocol and recordkeepers from the user. The application tier is the third tier:

Application		
Protocol		
Recordkeeper A	Recordkeeper B	Recordkeeper C
Ledger	Ledger	Ledger

For example, I send the bitcoin equivalent of $10 to my brother using the Bitcoin application. The bottom tier contains three copies of all of the Bitcoin transactions—that is, three copies of the ledger.

The middle tier contains the Bitcoin protocol, which allows the recordkeepers to communicate with each other in order to solve the puzzles to validate transactions.

The top tier contains the application for the automated transfer process. For example, Steve sending Gary the bitcoin equivalent of $10, Mary sending me two bitcoins, etc.

The Bitcoin application accepts the transaction and the protocol validates it. If the puzzle is solved by consensus among the recordkeepers, the $10 transfer is recorded in each ledger and is completed successfully.

If I try to send that same $10 to two people at the same time, called double-spending, the recordkeepers will work on solving the puzzles for both transactions. As soon as one of the puzzles is solved, that transaction will be accepted and recorded in the ledger, and the second transaction will be ignored.

To see actual Bitcoin transactions in action, visit www.Blockchain.info for the Bitcoin blockchain.

Again, these transactions are encrypted using public keys, so no one knows I am a cheap brother. Transactions are written to the ledger and stored in groups called "blocks." Each block is tied to the entry immediately prior to it—creating a chain. Hence the name "blockchain."

These three tiers of application, protocol, and ledger represent the blockchain architecture.

BLOCKCHAIN VARIATIONS

Blockchain applications can be described in terms of purpose and scope.

PURPOSE

Any application we build must serve a purpose and address one or more business requirements. A blockchain application could support one or more of these three purposes: currencies, contracts, or claims.

Currencies

Blockchain applications that focus on currency are digital accounting systems – ledgers which record money we send and receive. In our earlier example, the $10 I sent to my brother was transferred via Bitcoin.

There are hundreds of digital currency applications built using blockchain. The most popular blockchain currency application was also the first: Bitcoin. "Satoshi Nakamoto" wrote a whitepaper on the concepts of blockchain in 2008 and developed Bitcoin very shortly afterwards. The first Bitcoin transaction took place on January 3, 2009.[3]

By the way, the reason Satoshi's name is in quotes is because no one knows who Satoshi is, whether Satoshi is a male or female, in what part of the globe he/she resides, or even if Satoshi is one person or several. This is just one example of the mystique surrounding blockchain and digital currencies.

Recordkeeper computers in Bitcoin are called "miners." The unit of currency in Bitcoin is "bitcoin," or "coin" for short. To ensure bitcoins always have value, there is a finite number of bitcoins that can ever be mined. Similar to gold, having a finite supply means that if demand goes up, the price goes up too. We may not know how much

---

[3] http://bit.ly/2nuUR50.

gold is left in the earth to be mined, but we do know how many bitcoins.

Only 21 million bitcoins will ever exist. Why 21 million? Similar to the mystique behind Bitcoin's founder, no one knows for sure why the number 21 million was chosen. Some believe 21 million is a convenient amount to mathematically determine the mining rate. Others believe this number was chosen to align with the quantity of gold that has been mined: roughly 174,100 metric tons of gold have been mined since 2009, which if formed into a cube, would be 21 meters on a side. Still others tie it back to the classic, "Hitchhiker's Guide to the Galaxy," which proclaimed "42" as the answer to Life, the Universe, and Everything. 21 is half of 42, and this factors into the mathematical process behind the mining, where bitcoin rewards are halved every four years.[4]

When a miner solves a puzzle, the person or organization who owns that computer receives monetary compensation in bitcoins. This is how bitcoins are "mined." Tens of thousands of miners try to solve the cryptographic puzzles and there are incentives for doing so.

Contracts
Contract applications (also known as transactional applications) built in blockchain initiate and record

---

[4] http://bit.ly/2HHwvxZ.

transactions by invoking clauses in contracts. Agreements to purchase items or perform services are contracts. A purchase order for a book is a contract. If I agree to buy a book, there are payment and shipping transactions generated; all of these transactions can be stored in blockchain.

Blockchain applications invoke clauses in contracts through "smart contracts." Smart contracts are self-executed IF-THEN statements which can perform calculations, store information, or initiate movements of digital assets. If we characterize the activities documented in a contract, they can all be generalized as "IF-THEN" statements. If something is true, then do something else. The IF-THEN statements in our book purchase example include:

- If Steve orders the book, then he needs to pay for it.

- If Steve pays for the book, then we must ship it.

- If we ship the book, then we need to send the shipment tracking information.

- If we send Steve the tracking information, then we might send him a survey for him to rate our services.

- If Steve completes the survey, then we might send him a 10% off promotion for his next purchase.

A very powerful protocol for creating smart contracts is
Ethereum. Ethereum contains its own programming
language for building blockchain applications, and is
rapidly gaining popularity. Learn more at
http://www.ethereum101.org/.

UBS built a blockchain application to enforce contract
functionality in bonds. UBS records the bond's issuance,
interest calculation, coupon payments, and maturation
processes. When a bond becomes mature, a smart
contract initiates the principal payment to the bond
holder.[5]

Claims

In this context, "claims" are not insurance claims, but
instead ownership claims. We can record what people
and organizations own, including:

- Intellectual property

- Homes and vehicles

- Achievements

For example, I manage a publishing company. It is a
complex and expensive activity to register a book with
the Copyright office. However, it is necessary because it
stakes our claim to our work.

The US Copyright office could be considered one of those
"central power authorities" we discussed at the

---

[5] http://bit.ly/2oXN4vX.

beginning of this book. What if my publishing company wanted to avoid working with this monopoly of sorts? We could instead record the intellectual property rights using blockchain. We could take up to a 9-gig file representing our book and "hash" it into a 64-character blockchain address that is uniquely associated with that file. Since blockchain is immutable, once the hash was recorded at a certain time in blockchain, everyone would know that it was our intellectual property.

Creating an intellectual property registration system using blockchain might appear straightforward. However, there are other factors that need to be in place prior to making this registration process work. For example, can a copyright infringement case use a blockchain ledger as legal evidence? Widespread use of an intellectual property registration system using blockchain won't be feasible without significant progress in legal and government domains.

Technically, we can register any asset in the blockchain, and we as the owners have a private key associated with the asset. Eventually we can sell the asset and record the transaction in blockchain, and then someone else will own the asset with their own private key. For example, here is a ledger that records who owns a particular car:

Public key	Vehicle Identification Number (VIN)
983	4JGBF71E18A429191
123	SAJWA0HEXDMS56024
456	WP1AB29P88LA47599

From the prior example, we know my public key is 123. If I sell my vehicle to Bob whose public key is 983, this transaction in blockchain would get recorded as:

Recordkeeper A	
123	983
-SAJ	SAJ

Recordkeeper B	
123	983
-SAJ	SAJ

Recordkeeper C	
123	983
-SAJ	SAJ

Although I am only showing the first three letters of the VIN due to space on this page, and simplifying the sale using a minus sign, you can see that a transfer of ownership has taken place. There will need to be a money transaction that takes place before this transaction, however. I would need to first sell my car to Bob for $100:

Recordkeeper A	
123	983
$100	-$100

Recordkeeper B	
123	983
$100	-$100

Recordkeeper C	
123	983
$100	-$100

Smart contracts would need to be used to determine whether the VIN gets transferred to Bob. For example, IF Steve receives $100 from Bob, THEN transfer ownership to Bob.

Once the car is sold to Bob, his public key is now associated with the car's title and therefore the actual car.

"Attestation" refers to proof that something is true, including both "proof of existence" and "proof of ownership." Blockchain is a great platform for attestation services.

For example, the website https://poex.io/ creates hashes for documents and records these hashes in blockchain. The following was recorded for an early version of this book:

a05aac5e3ec2da3425f9c86764aaadb07ffe8b4345c9aba423042afcac8c34a1

This website does not require copying or uploading the document, as that would be a security issue. Instead, the document is hashed locally on your computer. This hashed key is associated with this and only this document. Then this key is stored in blockchain along with a timestamp, forever staking your claim to this document.

SCOPE

There are public and private blockchains.

A public blockchain is open to the world and is often called "permissionless." Anyone can view the ledger, use the application built on the ledger, and set up computers to act as recordkeepers for the ledger.

A private blockchain exists within an organization and is often called "permissioned." The organization owns the ledger, protocol, and application. Therefore, only employees of the organization (or those non-employees given access by the organization) can use the application and write to the ledger. Sometimes private blockchains are visible to the public (read-only), because there are only public keys and addresses visible, and therefore no security risks. A private blockchain is comparable to any other internal application built by an organization.

A variation of the private blockchain is the consortium blockchain. Instead of a single organization controlling and writing to the blockchain, a group of organizations control and write to the blockchain. For example, there might be a consortium of 50 financial institutions; as long as at least 35 validate a transaction, that transaction is written to the ledger. Only those members of the consortium can write to the blockchain application, but often the public can read the ledger—as there are no concerns with privacy due to public keys.

Applications should be built upon public blockchains when there is no need or want for users to be protected or controlled by a central power authority. Because private blockchains are controlled by one or more organizations, this can put a real (or perceived) limit on the freedom given by blockchain. As such, build applications on public blockchains whenever possible.

Of course, this is not always possible. Applications should be built upon private blockchains when there is a need to:

- **Know the users**. There are situations where an organization or consortium has additional resources to confirm whether the data can be trusted. In these specific cases, it is not sufficient for the owner(s) to write the data to the ledger.

The owners also need to validate the ledger against other internal data. For example, consider a blockchain application that is designed to settle equity trades among organizations in a certain consortium. In this case, one (or more) of the owning organizations must confirm that the person placing the trade has an account with one of the organizations in the consortium.

- **Know the recordkeepers.** If anyone can set up recordkeepers, anyone has the ability to own enough recordkeepers to form a majority. At this point, it becomes possible for someone to enter an invalid transaction, but own enough recordkeepers to have them approve it. Assume that someone owns 51% of the recordkeepers that validate a trade, and places a trade for 100 shares of IBM. With the majority in place, the owner can approve the trade—even though no payment was received.

- **Perform.** In private blockchains, fewer recordkeepers are needed to validate a transaction, because there is a greater degree of trust placed on the users. Fewer recordkeepers to validate a transaction means less time is needed to process a transaction, therefore leading to improved performance.

- **Save the environment.** Blockchain is very hard on the environment. Recordkeepers are computers that use electricity to power and cool; as such, thousands of recordkeepers can take a toll on the environment. For example, in the Bitcoin network, the combined electricity used by the miners is 350 megawatts—roughly equivalent to the electricity demand of 280,000 American households.[6] With fewer recordkeepers in a private blockchain, less energy is used.

SUMMARY

Many buzzwords in technology, including blockchain, carry ambiguous definitions. Sometimes the term "blockchain" refers to the actual ledger, sometimes to the protocol, sometimes to the application, and sometimes to all three tiers. In the spirit of precision, in this book blockchain is the ledger. The blockchain architecture refers to all three tiers of application, protocol, and ledger.

The ledger tier is managed by the recordkeepers. The protocol tier provides the language for transaction validation among recordkeepers and the invoking of smart contracts, which are IF-THEN statements. The application tier automates one or more business processes to enhance a user experience.

---

[6] http://bit.ly/2iVMblX.

We can use blockchain applications without divulging private information about ourselves, through the use of public keys and addresses.

A blockchain application supports one or more of these three purposes: Currencies, Contracts, and Claims. Blockchain applications that focus on currency are digital accounting systems—ledgers which record money we send and receive. Contract applications built in blockchain initiate and record transactions by invoking clauses in contracts. Claims applications capture ownership.

There are both public and private blockchains. A public blockchain allows anyone to view the ledger, use the application built on the ledger, and set up computers to act as recordkeepers for the ledger. A private blockchain exists within an organization, and the organization owns the ledger, protocol, and application.

Now that the concepts of blockchain have been discussed, let's move on to the principles of usage.

PART II

Blockchain Usage

Many existing applications in our organizations could be replaced or enhanced by incorporating shared immutable ledgers. In addition, blockchain applications can be built for processes that are today performed manually.

This section will explore the tremendous potential of these different uses for blockchain, with an emphasis on patterns. Patterns are templates, concepts, or ideas noticed in one area that can be applied to other areas.

Patterns are very useful, as they save us future work. In my data modeling work, for example, employees, students, and consumers are all people of interest to most organizations. These groups of people exhibit similar behaviors (such as breathing and laughing), and have similar properties (such as names and birth dates). We can generalize the behaviors and properties of employees, students, and consumers into the pattern of "Person." Once we understand and design for "Person," we can build more extensible and integrated databases, gracefully accommodating additional types of people, such as contractors and instructors.

Remember the theme in this book: if you understand the concepts and principles behind a technology, you'll be able to apply it intelligently. The concepts were covered in Part I and the principles in the form of patterns will be covered in Part II.

There are three important types of patterns in blockchain: requirements patterns, risk patterns, and process patterns.

REQUIREMENTS PATTERNS

Once we understand the requirements patterns, we can fit them to any industry; this helps us identify opportunities for usage. Although the possibilities for using blockchain are virtually countless, five common patterns emerge as the most common. These five patterns truly drive blockchain development.

This overview will explain the five patterns, and each chapter in this section will show an actual use case for each of these five patterns within a particular industry: finance, insurance, government, manufacturing, retail, utilities, healthcare, nonprofit, publishing, music, and art.

We do not cover an exhaustive list of industries, or of usages within each industry. Use the following chapters to generate ideas; start from our examples and figure out how you can apply blockchain within your organization.

There might be blockchain applications already available for some of these usages. For other usages, you might be in uncharted territory, leading the charge to improve your organization's processes with blockchain.

The reason for building a blockchain application must be for at least one of these five requirements patterns: transparency, streamlining, privacy, permanence, or distribution.

TRANSPARENCY

Transparency means that a user, consumer, or organization has visibility into an entire process—not just the end result.

Did you know, for example, that 80% of the Italian olive oil on the market is fraudulent? Even though that label in the supermarket might say "extra virgin" or "Italian," the olive oil can be very poor quality and come from other countries such as Syria, Turkey, and Morocco.[7]

So if we can't trust the label on an item we purchase, how do we know the item is what it says it is? We can purchase olive oil directly from the source, but there is time and expense in traveling to a local farm in Italy.

Another option is having proof that supports the claims on the label. In other words, if we can have transparency of a production and supply chain process, we can see where the product was made and validate claims made by the manufacturer or seller.

For example, if you were shopping in the supermarket and wanted to confirm that the extra virgin Italian olive oil in your hand was indeed that, there could be a

---

[7] http://bit.ly/2oq9aba.

barcode or QR code on the package. You could scan it with your smartphone, and an app would show you the production lineage of your bottle, starting with that family farm in Puglia.

Each leg of the production journey can be recorded in the blockchain, providing the immutable ledger we need to feel comfortable purchasing a product.

Transparency can confirm any characteristic of importance, such as gluten, organic, or peanut-free. Transparency gives us lineage visibility which can lead to a reduction in corruption, fraud, or waste, and an increase in trust. In your industry, look for processes that have little to no visibility and a lack of stakeholder trust.

STREAMLINING

Streamlining means making existing processes more efficient, saving time and money. Streamlining involves removing intermediaries, leading to quicker transaction times, fewer steps, and lower fees.

Imagine that I invent a new ice cream flavor called Peanut Butter Frog. Peanut Butter Frog ice cream is something I believe will be successful, so I start the lengthy patent process. This process can take years, and cost thousands of dollars. One way to streamline this process would be to register my invention using blockchain. I would then have an immutable place to stake my claim, and announcing my invention would take minutes instead of years. In your industry, look for lengthy complex business processes, and see if they can be made faster and cheaper using blockchain.

PRIVACY

Privacy means participating in a process without divulging sensitive information. With blockchain, we can use public keys and addresses to represent ourselves and our transactions. No private information, such as social security numbers or credit card numbers, travel over the internet. Someone can buy a scoop of Peanut Butter Frog ice cream and pay using Bitcoin, and we will never know the identity of the consumer. In your industry, look for processes that have the opportunity to expose sensitive information, and see if they can be replaced using blockchain.

PERMANENCE

If information has permanence, it is stored forever in an easily accessible format. There is no need to search through filing cabinets, hard drives, or spreadsheets to locate a document from six years ago.

If some business owner were audited for tax deductions, and suddenly needed proof that she bought her staff an ice cream party three years ago and wrote it off as an expense, her receipt would still be safely stored in the ledger, and the purchase could be verified. In your industry, look for documents and transactions that need to be stored and retrieved over a long period of time.

DISTRIBUTION

Distribution means that many people or computers are involved in completing a transaction. For example, if my ownership claim to the Peanut Butter Frog flavor is stored on twenty computers, and a hurricane wipes out five of them, my claim is still safely stored. In your industry, look for scenarios where having multiple recordkeepers would be advantageous, such as minimizing risk or generating new opportunities.

RISK PATTERNS

In addition to identifying blockchain requirements patterns, there are also risk patterns. We can recognize the obstacles in our path and propose general solutions.

COOPERATION

Blockchain applications often require organizations to interact directly with each other, rather than interacting with an intermediary. We know how difficult it can be to get different departments within our organization to work together. Imagine the difficulty in convincing people to work together across organizations. It could be possible for standards organizations to facilitate this cooperation.

INCENTIVES

There must exist incentives to work together. If the organizations benefit from having that intermediary in place, why should the process change? For example, one of the processes we will discuss in the media chapter is the royalty payment process. Blockchain allows us to pay royalties to authors minutes after a sale, instead of up to six months later. What incentives, however, would a publisher or distributor have for paying their authors in a shorter timeframe?

CHANGE

There is always risk with trying something new. How do we know that processes will improve with blockchain? Blockchain requires a different mindset—one that is comfortable with shared control and transparency instead of centralized power and opaque processes. It can be scary to make the leap to blockchain. Change is often scary.

PROCESS PATTERNS

One of my favorite books on business processes is *How Work Gets Done*, by Artie Mahal. On page 30 of his book, Artie defines the term "business process" and provides a powerful visualization:

> The simple definition of a business process is: "how work gets done." It is a series of activities or tasks that are performed together to produce a defined result. Typically, a process has inputs which are transformed into outputs and outcomes.

The following explanation of Inputs, Outputs, Guides, and Enablers is excerpted with permission from *How Work Gets Done*, pages 56-59. Grab a copy of *How Work Gets Done* if you'd like to learn more about processes.

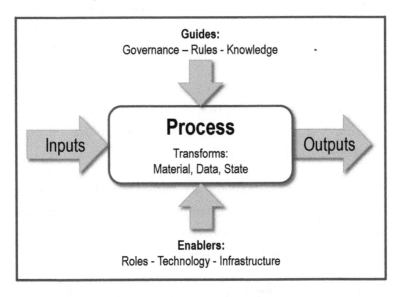

A process is initiated by an *Event*. It receives *Inputs*, which are transformed into *Outputs*. The transformation uses *Guides* to manage and control the process, and *Enablers* (such as human resources, systems, data, and infrastructure) to support execution of the process.

Inputs are provided by stakeholders and/or upstream business processes. They may be raw material, data, or any other resource that the process will transform into output. The input source may be internal or external to the organization. Consider the example of placing an order for a book. The data about the customer, book, and payment amount becomes actionable information only after a user or process feeds it into the purchase process.

Inputs are transformed by the process into outputs. Outputs are the deliverables and goals of a process. For example, the finished product is produced, the book is sold, or the insurance claim is paid.

Guides manage and control the transformation of inputs into their planned outputs. Unlike inputs, which are consumed or transformed by the process, guides are only referenced—not consumed.

An organization's enablers are those reusable resources that are engaged in supporting the process. If the guides are the *rules*, the enablers are the *tools*. Enablers can be classified into three categories:

- **Human Capital**. Roles represent the jobs or positions assigned to execute a process. This is the critical people-process link. The skills and competencies required to execute the process are used to define role profiles that, in turn, become job descriptions.

- **Enabling Technology**. Technology is a broad term covering a variety of mechanisms that provide technical support to processes. This includes business application systems, data stores, IT tools and platforms, production lines, and general tools.

- **Supporting Infrastructure.** The term
  "infrastructure" covers a variety of platforms and
  foundations upon which the enablers function.
  For people, infrastructure includes work space,
  buildings, and energy. For systems, it includes
  hardware, software, and communications
  platforms.

BLOCKCHAIN IMPACTS ENABLERS

Recall our ongoing discussion of central power
authorities and monopolies, which often act as
intermediaries in highly-regulated processes. In most of
these processes, we must trust that these intermediaries
will complete the process in an accurate and timely
fashion. As such, the central power authority is an
enabler of the process.

As we've mentioned, one of the overarching features of
blockchain is that it doesn't require much
intermediation. As we will see in the chapters that follow,
blockchain applications often remove or redefine the
enabler acting as an intermediary. The guides remain the
same. The only thing that blockchain changes is how
these rules are executed and how the data is stored.

In the following chapters, we will use the patterns
mentioned in this overview to illustrate how blockchain
can assist many areas of our organizations. For each of
the five requirements processes (transparency,

streamlining, privacy, permanence, and distribution) of blockchain, we will choose one example process that is typical to the industry in question. We'll then walk through the process and explore the ways in which blockchain could supplement or improve it. We will also highlight risk patterns where appropriate.

CHAPTER 2

Blockchain within Finance

TRANSPARENCY

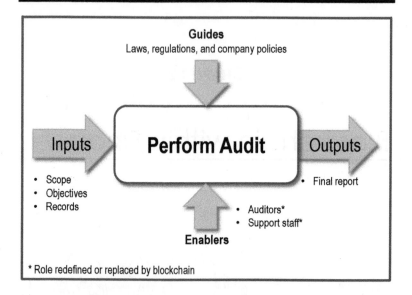

The audit process begins by determining the scope of the audit—the organization, process, department, or system to be reviewed.

Next, the objectives of the audit are communicated. These include confirming accounting practices, streamlining processes, or improving system effectiveness.

Knowing the scope and objectives helps us hone in on the records needed as input for the audit. The audit must follow the rules set forth in laws, regulations, and company policies.

The auditors invest time in reviewing the records and meeting with support staff and other employees, in order to complete the audit. Once the audit is complete, the results are documented.

A blockchain application of this process will contain a ledger of all of the records by date, making the auditing process much more automated (rather than manually searching through digital files on multiple computers, or rummaging through paper documentation). Smart contracts can be used to proactively create timely auditing reports and email them to management, regulators, and auditors.

Auditing costs companies a fortune today. The average hourly fee for auditing services was over $150 in 2017.[8]

Blockchain can save organizations billions of dollars by storing relevant input data in the ledger and using smart contracts to automatically produce periodic reports.

A blockchain application of this process will require cooperation among organizations, auditors, and tax collectors.

---

[8] http://bit.ly/2emHbEU.

STREAMLINING

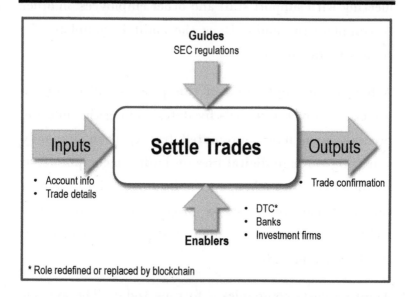

To settle a trade, we need the buyer's or seller's account information, plus the trade details. Banks, investment firms, and the Depository Trust Company (DTC) can all participate in settling a trade. When someone places an order for 100 shares of IBM stock, the trade confirmation is not received until the settlement process is complete.

The Depository Trust Company (DTC) is ultimately responsible for making sure the transaction is completed safely and securely.

The DTC acts as a clearinghouse to process and settle trades in corporate and municipal securities. In addition to safekeeping, recordkeeping, and clearing services, the

DTC provides direct registration, underwriting, reorganization, and proxy and dividend services.[9]

It can take days for this trusted intermediary to validate the process, acting as a clearing agent. All communication with the DTC takes place through brokers, banks, and settlement agents—each also acting as intermediaries for related processes. I worked on Wall Street when we went from settling a trade in five days to three. It was a major accomplishment.

In 2014, settling a trade went from three days to two days, but that still is a lot of time. It is expensive, too; settling trades in the financial industry costs upwards of $80 billion a year globally.[10]

By using blockchain technology and removing or redefining the role of the DTC in the process, trades can take as little as ten minutes and cost pennies.

In addition, all of the details associated with trades are stored in the ledger, instead of using costly archival methods (including paper).

There is currently substantial effort being invested into building a blockchain application in this area, but success will require lots of cooperation among banks, investment firms, and the DTC.

---

[9] http://bit.ly/2Fq2HEc.
[10] http://bit.ly/2DIhzy1.

PRIVACY

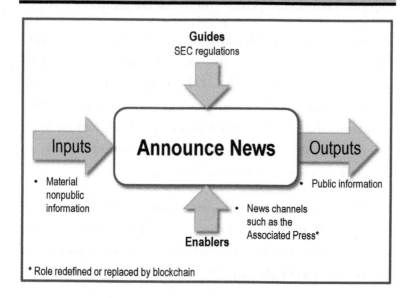

Insider trading is the buying or selling of a security by someone who has access to material, nonpublic information about the security. Insider trading can be illegal or legal, depending on when the insider makes the trade. It is illegal when the material information is still nonpublic.[11] For example, if someone has news that will most likely make IBM stock skyrocket, and they buy the stock before this news is made public, that is illegal. However, if they announce the news, or wait until the news is announced before buying the stock, that is legal.

A blockchain application can be used to minimize insider trading. The person can easily post (or have someone post) the news via blockchain, and it remains

---

[11] http://bit.ly/2FCpw7D.

anonymous, yet creates a permanent record of when the story was posted. The person can then immediately buy or sell the stock legally, as the trade will be made after the story was posted.

A challenge with posting news from anonymous sources is that it creates an incentive to spread "fake news," which are false stories that appear to be factual news, spread on the internet or using other media.[12] Imagine someone posting fake news about IBM and how that might impact the IBM stock price.

PERMANENCE

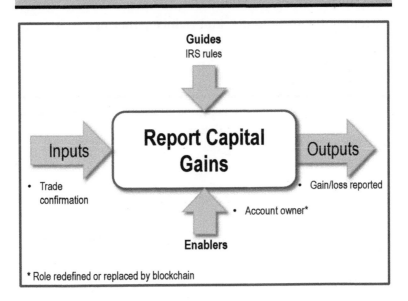

When someone sells a stock, often there is a gain or loss that must be reported for tax purposes. A few years ago, I was switching brokerage firms and moving my stocks to the new firm. When I traded those stocks, I needed to report capital gains on my tax form. However, I bought the stocks so long ago that it took me hours to find the paper trade statements; I was glad that I still had them at all!

A blockchain trading system will record when every buy and sell transaction occurred. Furthermore, using a smart contract to initiate a capital gains summary of the trade would make the whole capital gains process automated. This would save people hours of time searching for statements, and reduce paper usage.

DISTRIBUTION

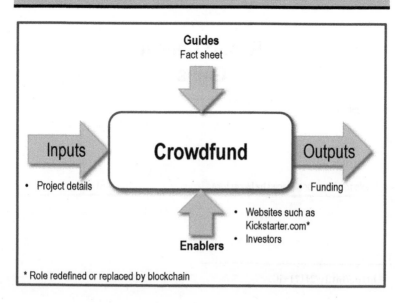

Crowdfunding is a process of raising money for a project through lots of small investments from many people. There are intermediaries today that facilitate crowdfunding, such as Kickstarter and Indiegogo.

Blockchain allows companies to crowdfund without these intermediaries. Startups can create their own digital currency in blockchain; the currency is equivalent to shares in the company, which can be sold to investors.

Startups such as Swarm, Koinify, and Lighthouse have raised millions using this blockchain approach.[13]

---

[13] http://bit.ly/2mURg0D.

CHAPTER 3

Blockchain within Insurance

TRANSPARENCY

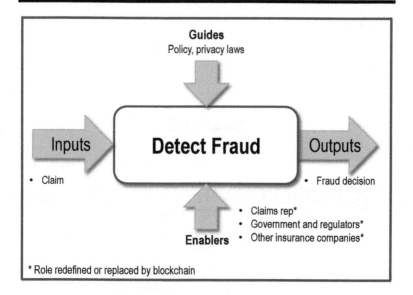

Once a claim is filed, checks must be performed to ensure the claim is not fraudulent. A blockchain application can be built to detect and reduce fraud, by storing and allowing access to relevant documents such as medical records, police reports, and prior claims history.

Since the blockchain is immutable, it can be trusted to store preexisting conditions by date. For example, if a car already has a big dent and then a claim is filed, and that dent is part of the claim, the claims representative can check the immutable history and confirm that the dent was already there before.

Using blockchain for fraud detection works for other types of insurance as well. For example, if someone has a preexisting health condition that is recorded in the ledger, and then that person switches health insurance companies, it is possible that the new insurance company can access the ledger and be able to view information on that preexisting condition.

However, this requires looking beyond the boundaries of your insurance company. Cooperation among insurance companies and other organizations (including governments and regulators) is necessary, as information must be shared to detect fraud. Also, privacy laws such as HIPPA must be obeyed.

STREAMLINING

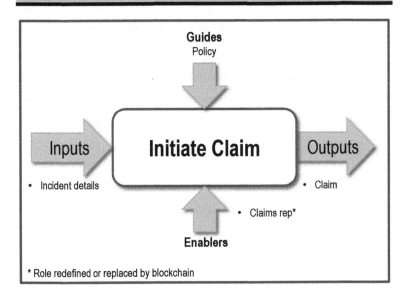

Have you ever filed an insurance claim? You know the process, then. It can be as enjoyable as a visit to the dentist. Long phone calls, lots of transfers, and many follow-up calls. Blockchain can lead to the automatic initiation of claims, instead of having someone call and talk with a claims representative.

Connecting the Internet of Things (IoT) with blockchain, for example, can lead to blockchain smart contracts being embedded in devices. These devices can automatically file a claim and even initiate the repair process. If someone is in a car accident, for example, the smart contract can detect that an accident occurred through sensors in the car, and then initiate the claim and even schedule an appointment with the body mechanic. Another example deals with airline flight insurance. There is a start-up that created an application for flight insurance companies, to automatically initiate claim payouts when flights are cancelled or delayed. There is no lengthy claims process or claims representative involvement. Everything happens automatically.

One of the challenges of attempting to automate this process with blockchain is the lack of incentive. Insurance companies may be paying claims out sooner than anticipated. On the other hand, claims will be closed sooner than anticipated, which can be a good thing for insurance companies—the longer claims are open, the more expensive they can get.

PRIVACY

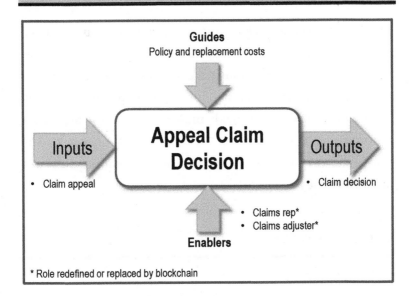

Sometimes an appeal is filed when a claim decision is made. I went through this process with Hurricane Sandy years ago. The insurance company gave us a very low initial claim settlement amount that was not going to cover even half of the repairs. We hired a claims adjuster who did a lot of research and worked with the insurance company to come up with a settlement amount that would cover most of our repairs. It was a lengthy and stressful process.

Using blockchain, the claims adjuster (or possibly even the policyholder), can have access to prior claims settlements in the same geographic area, by multiple insurance companies, and thereby make more informed decisions. It is also possible for the claims representative to have access to this information and make the original claim settlement more accurate.

The key question is the same as in the previous process: what incentive would insurance companies have for transitioning to blockchain? Also, what incentives would claims adjustors have for participating? Using blockchain for claim appeals makes the process more of a commodity type service, which could increase the competition in the adjuster community, leading to lower rates that they receive.

PERMANENCE

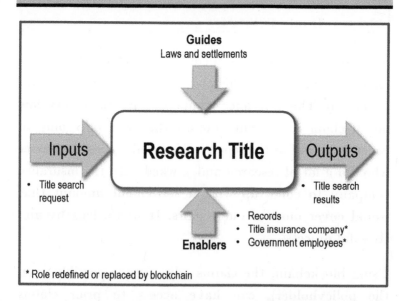

A very large cost in purchasing property is title insurance. Title insurance is insurance that mortgage organizations require the homeowner to purchase in order to protect the property's title from liens. A lien is a charge upon real or personal property for the satisfaction of some debt or duty ordinarily arising by operation of law.[14]

The title insurance company researches the property to make sure there are no liens. They are willing to provide insurance because they believe there are no surprises, such as a long-lost cousin of the previous homeowner proving they own the property.

I had to do a title search myself recently, and I was shocked by how paper-driven and error-prone the process was.

If all of the title information can be stored in blockchain, the process can become automated. This takes less time and increases accuracy, removing the need for title insurance.

---

[14] http://bit.ly/2DWaQ2S.

DISTRIBUTION

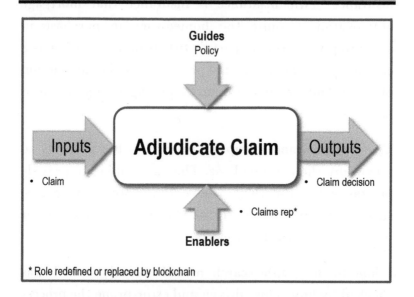

Adjudication is an insurance industry phrase for the process of paying or denying claims after comparing them to the benefit or coverage requirements.[15]

Blockchain can validate and automate the claims process. The rules between claim and policy can be embedded in the blockchain by use of smart contracts. For example, if there is a rule that a car only be fixed by an approved mechanic, this can be programmed into a blockchain contract. Other rules could include, for instance, prohibiting two claims from the same claimant for the same incident, or ensuring the claim is for a valid policy.

---

[15] http://bit.ly/2ExERHd.

For a minor car accident, for example, it could be possible for a claimant to take pictures of the car and upload them through the web to a blockchain application. The application will validate the claimant's information to ensure that they are a valid policyholder.

The claims representative could view the pictures online and approve the claim, triggering blockchain smart contracts to automate the payment.

CHAPTER 4

Blockchain within Government

TRANSPARENCY

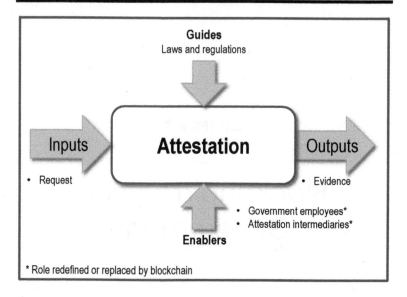

Documents and services focused on proving that something is true—such as notary services, licenses, and permits—rely on processes of attestation. Today these processes of attestation are heavily people-intensive, error-prone, and relatively expensive.

A blockchain application focused on attestation would record information about the actual event or document, along with date information. This immutable record provides proof of existence. With this relatively simple act, we can remove or redirect certain government agencies and intermediaries (such as notaries) in the attestation process.

For example, there already exists a service called Virtual Notary which provides a certificate, which is a hash of an actual file such as an email, statement, or contract. These supporting files can be in any format, such as Microsoft Word, PDF, JPG, or even PowerPoint.

A blockchain application for attestation would make "proof of existence" and "proof of ownership" a more self-serve process. Citizens would invoke smart contracts to perform services that today are carried out by government agencies or attestation intermediaries.

STREAMLINING

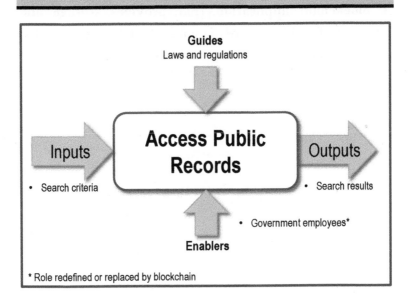

I recently had to go to my county's Hall of Records to obtain some information on a deed. The process was so people-intensive. Not to mention all of the space needed for the aisles and aisles of large red binders that contained paper records dating back to 1794!

A blockchain application could make it much easier for citizens to access public records. All of the public documents mentioned earlier under the Transparency section could be easily accessed without reliance on a government intermediary.

Delaware is currently moving its states archival records to blockchain.[16] Several countries including Dubai are also moving their paper storage and retrieval systems to blockchain.[17]

A blockchain application that provides storage and retrieval of public records is equivalent to a distributed and easily accessible content management system.

---

[16] http://bit.ly/2DtTXPV.

[17] http://bit.ly/2FL5rMH.

PRIVACY

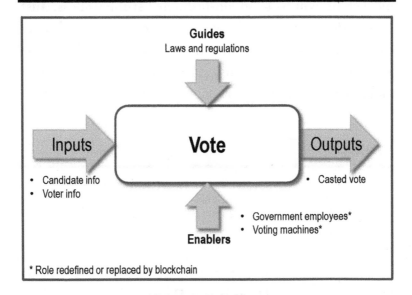

Most electronic voting systems today are centralized. Therefore, the company that built the voting software has a powerful intermediary role, and could theoretically influence election results.

With blockchain, the clunky voting machines and software are gone. Voting transactions are recorded in the immutable ledger and can be automatically tallied using smart contracts.

There is a startup called Follow My Vote that is building the first online voting software based on blockchain technology.[18]

---

[18] http://bit.ly/1Bhm1PC.

The biggest challenge with moving the voting process to blockchain will be good old-fashioned stubbornness. Just like with any new process, most voters will be more comfortable voting the way they always have. A simple graphical user interface and short training tutorials could make the transition easier.

PERMANENCE

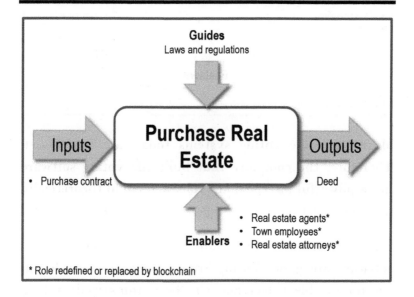

The current process to purchase real estate (e.g. a house or land) is incredibly paper-intensive and prone to error. So many people are involved, such as real estate agents, town employees in departments such as zoning and building codes, and real estate attorneys. With so many people involved and lots of money at stake, buying real estate can be a very stressful process.

A blockchain application can help by storing all relevant documents in one step, in an immutable format. Smart contracts could be used as process management tools, to quickly start one process when another finishes. This type of application is a workflow application—a perfect fit for blockchain.

Documentation (including land registries, zoning violations, and property titles) can be stored in the blockchain ledger for easy access. Ghana is one of the countries that has implemented a land registry system using blockchain, in order to prevent corruption and foul play.[19]

Sweden is working on a system to place real estate transactions using blockchain so that buyers, sellers, and financial institutions can track the real estate purchase process.[20]

---

[19] http://bit.ly/2BfWFU0.
[20] http://bit.ly/2nvTgtw.

DISTRIBUTION

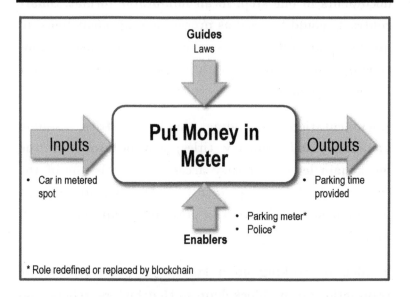

There is a town near me where parking is an issue, and therefore many parking spots have meters. People put money in the meters and are given a certain amount of time to park. If the time lapses this person could be given a parking ticket.

I parked recently at a metered spot, and had only two quarters, which gave me 40 minutes. My appointment lasted closer to an hour, so in addition to the stress of rushing to my car, I worried if I would receive a ticket.

A blockchain application can definitely help in this process. Someone parks a car in a metered spot. The meter scans a QR code which represents the person's digital currency address. The person is then charged to park. The person is charged for the duration of the parking event. No more running out of time in a meter, or feeding the meter with extra coins and leaving the parking spot with money in the meter.

Yet again, though, incentive would prove a challenge. What incentive would municipalities have for switching to a metering blockchain application? Currently, many towns make substantial revenue off of tickets, and this application would remove tickets altogether. However, salaries would be saved, because the police would not have to monitor meters.

CHAPTER 5

Blockchain within Manufacturing and Retail

TRANSPARENCY

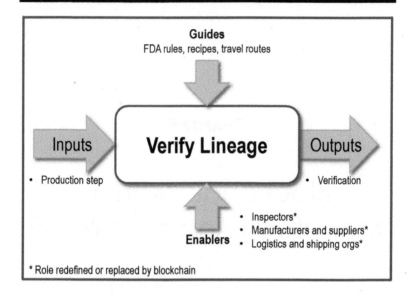

We can use blockchain to keep track of product lineage, from raw materials through to finished products, as well as for tracking packages through legs of the journey.

At every point in the manufacturing process, we can record both characteristics and responsible party information in the ledger. Characteristics include organic, farm-raised, environment-friendly, Kosher, Halal, gluten free, recycled material, and made with renewable energy. Responsible parties are those that own one or more steps in the manufacturing process, or are responsible for a transportation segment.

Knowing every step along the way has its advantages. For example, if you order wild salmon in a restaurant, it should be possible to track it down to where it was caught and whether it was from a sustainable source. If organic carrots are purchased, we should be able to identify the farm.

The idea of confirming the "catch to plate" lineage might sound farfetched, but it is being done today. Viant and the World Wild Fund for Nature partnered to provide a blockchain application to do just this.[21]

A blockchain application focusing on lineage also includes shipping. The recipient of a shipment can check status, and port officials can access shipment information as well.

Containers, pallets, and trailers can all be associated with smart contracts that record arrivals, departures, or change of custody in the blockchain ledger.

Marine Transport International Ltd., a U.K.-based freight forwarder, is using blockchain for this purpose. The blockchain application replaces lots of spreadsheets and other types of documents that usually only exist on someone's desktop.

Jody Cleworth, the company's chief executive officer, calls blockchain a "natural fit" for shipping, which involves compiling and transmitting complex data sets

---

[21] http://for.tn/2CxD5rb.

between "so many participants, suppliers and regulatory organizations."[22]

One such dataset relevant to shipping is the Bill of Lading document. This document contains proof of ownership as shipments pass along the chain from party to party, such as from exporter to shipper to importer. Storing this document in blockchain would have a lot of great benefits.

Generalizing the concept of shipping, there are a number of blockchain efforts to better track lineage in transportation. The Blockchain in Transport Alliance (BiTA) has many members in the field of transportation, and is working through standards and use cases for blockchain within the industry.[23]

One of the most significant challenges with creating a blockchain application to track lineage is the buy-in. An effective process would demand a large amount of cooperation from organizations involved in every part of the manufacturing or shipping process, as well as from government port authorities. Hopefully the BiTA can facilitate these arrangements and make cooperation easier.

---

[22] http://on.wsj.com/2dhvLQk.
[23] http://bit.ly/2BHNlx9.

STREAMLINING

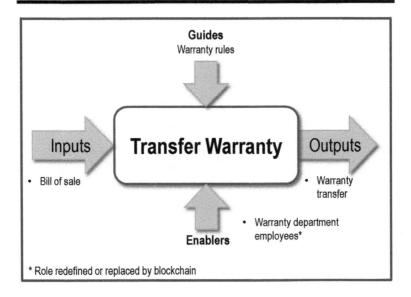

Wouldn't it be great to buy a used product that is still under warranty and have the warranty automatically be transferred to you? It could be anything from a toaster to a car. Blockchain can make this process seamless. By storing warranty information, a product sale can initiate a smart contract that will transfer the warranty quickly and painlessly to the purchaser.

There is currently a blockchain service called Warranteer where consumers can maintain warranty information for products purchased, and even transfer them when the product is sold.

PRIVACY

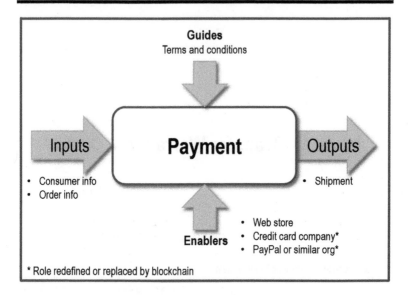

Today when we buy something online, our payment details (i.e. credit card numbers) are being stored somewhere, along with our names and addresses. Blockchain hides all this, so that only public keys and addresses are available. As such, the transaction process is much more secure.

We can purchase an item and not worry about our identity being stolen. In addition, instead of organizations paying very high fees for credit card or PayPal purchases, the equivalent of pennies can be paid using a digital currency such as Bitcoin.

PERMANENCE

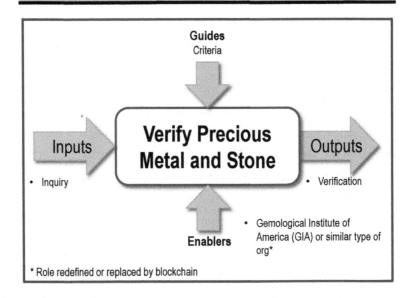

I bought diamond earrings for my wife's birthday many years ago. I did a lot of research on diamonds and spent several days haggling with diamond dealers in Manhattan's diamond district. My wife lost one of the earrings about two years later and I went through a similar process to replace it. Last summer she lost another earring, and about a month ago I again went through a similar process to replace it.

Apart from the adrenaline rush of haggling with diamond experts much more skilled at negotiating then me, another source of stress was the nagging thought that *maybe the diamond I am buying is not what the dealer says it is.* A piece of paper can say anything. It can claim that the diamond weighs 1.2 carats when the diamond actually weighs .99. It can lie about the color and clarity as well.

Blockchain is making inroads in the area of precious metals and diamonds, to increase transparency and make sure the purchaser is getting what the salesperson claims they are getting. Not only does this lead to more confidence during the buying process, it also can make us feel better ethically. Many diamonds are mined and traded in areas under conflict, and these diamonds fund war and corruption. The purchaser would be able to see if the diamonds in consideration are these so-called "blood diamonds."

Bruce Cleaver is the CEO of De Beers Group, which has 35% control of the world's diamond market.[24] According to Cleaver, "Diamonds hold enduring value and represent some of life's most meaningful moments, so it's essential to provide assurance that a diamond is conflict-free and natural. By leveraging blockchain technology, we will provide an additional layer of assurance to consumers and industry participants, with every diamond registered on the platform having a record as everlasting as the diamond itself."[25]

During the grading process, De Beers Group inscribes each diamond over .16 carats with a unique identifier. This identifier can be cross-referenced using blockchain.

---

[24] http://bit.ly/2eFSoDX.
[25] http://bit.ly/2rrnB3E.

Diamonds are forever, and so is the blockchain ledger.

The process of identifying an item and providing a complete and immutable lineage of that item's history is not just limited to diamonds. It can be used for valuables including gold, watches, art, and antiques. These processes are currently antiquated and often paper-based, easily susceptible to forgery and foul play.

One challenge to using blockchain for precious stone and metal verification is that a trusted intermediary will still need to exist (as an enabler) to validate the item. For example, when De Beers Group inscribes the diamonds, they act as a trusted intermediary providing a service for this blockchain application.

DISTRIBUTION

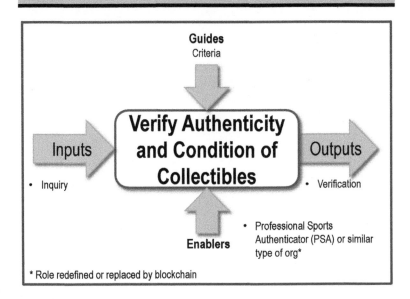

In addition to diamonds, we can also validate the authenticity and condition of collectibles. I used to be a big baseball card collector. In the early 1990s the entire baseball card industry tanked, and it still has not recovered. Part of the reason is that it is so easy to counterfeit cards.

Baseball cards are validated by several organizations, such as the Professional Sports Authenticator (PSA). Unfortunately, this process is costly and (some claim) subjective and prone to error.

What if each baseball card could exist in a plastic protector containing a small QR code, which represents its blockchain address? This code could be scanned to learn about its condition and other important information.

CHAPTER 6

Blockchain within Utilities

TRANSPARENCY

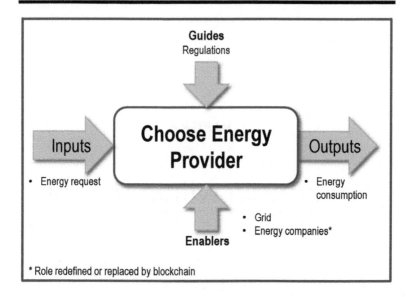

In many markets, utilities are some of the last true monopolies. We turn on lights, computers, and appliances, and receive our monthly electric or gas bill. However, just as phone companies blossomed in the late 1980s, regulations are now opening the utility market to more companies. New technologies (like smart meters, blockchain, and IoT sensor readings) combined with the availability of alternate energy sources (such as sun and wind), are lowering entry costs for these companies to compete, giving consumers many more diverse energy choices.

A blockchain application can store information provided by sensors that precisely measure how much energy is being used and when the energy is being consumed. This will aid the consumer in making intelligent energy selection choices, with full knowledge of factors such as cost and source.

STREAMLINING

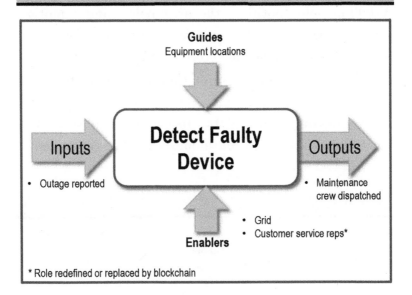

When a device in a utility's network breaks, it is frequently reported by the person or organization who is immediately impacted by the loss of service. If a tree falls taking down electrical wires, for example, usually it is up to the homeowner impacted by the fallen tree to report the outage.

If we could combine IoT sensor technology with blockchain, however, the device in need of repair (or nearby devices) could initiate a smart contract to record the trouble ticket. Blockchain would be used as a decentralized ledger where devices in disperse geographic areas could write to it, and consumer representatives and maintenance crews could react.

The startup Filament does this today by installing sensor devices on power poles in the Australian outback. A falling pole "notifies" the next pole using a motion sensor. If that pole does not record the activity in the ledger, the next pole will record it, and so on—for up to ten miles away. With tens of thousands of smart poles collecting data through numerous sensors and communicating that data to another device, the blockchain application continuously tracks everything.[26]

PRIVACY

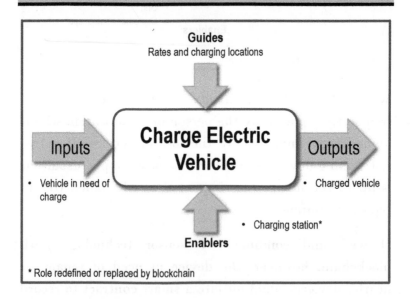

---

[26] http://for.tn/1rNTCOG.

I own an electric car, and the process of charging it when I travel is not always easy or private. I sometimes feel that when I plug in the charger, "Big Brother" is watching and knows exactly where I am. Sure, I sometimes keep Location Services on in my phone, but sometimes it is nice not to be tracked.

With blockchain, the account information when charging can be kept encrypted. Therefore, cars can be charged without divulging private information such as identification or location.

PERMANENCE

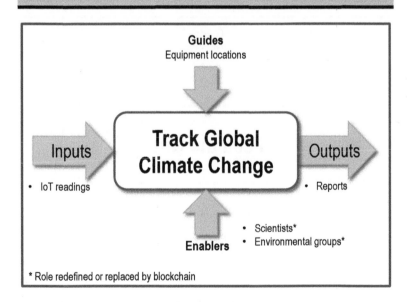

Sensor and other IoT readings can be stored in blockchain. Because the data is immutable, scientists and environmental groups can more easily track long-term changes in the environment.

In addition, smart contracts can trigger alerts. For example, if the ozone layer over a particular area becomes less than a certain thickness, an emergency alert will automatically be sent to a government official.

Being immutable and being factual means it might be easier to gain support from citizens and politicians for environmental initiatives.

DISTRIBUTION

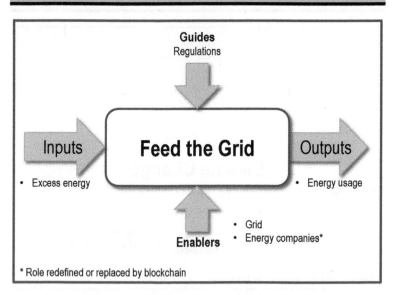

The transparency example at the start of this chapter explored consumers having more choices in energy providers. Here we explore the process from the energy provider perspective.

It is possible that with a blockchain application, anyone with a source of power can feed the grid. For example, a homeowner with solar panels on their roof can "sell" their excess electricity to the grid. The selling and accounting would be performed in blockchain.

Solar Change is doing this today by offering their own currency, SolarCoins, in exchange for energy. Brooklyn Microgrid is also doing something similar, with a community microgrid. This will allow residents to buy and sell energy they produce from rooftop solar power installations, using the existing energy infrastructure and the blockchain ledger for recording and accounting purposes.[27]

---

[27] http://bit.ly/2nSogqx.

CHAPTER 7

Blockchain within Healthcare

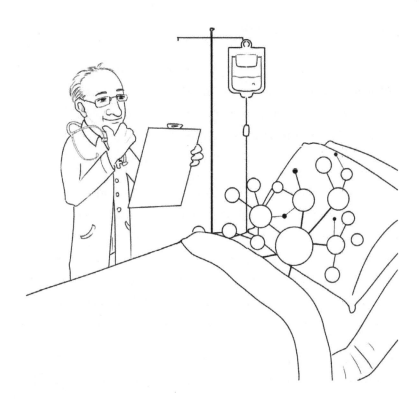

TRANSPARENCY

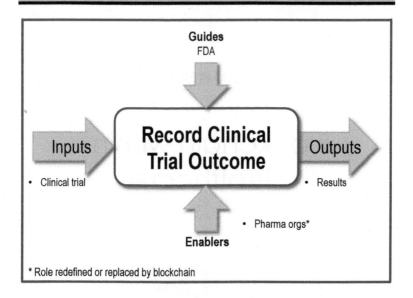

The process of performing clinical trials is lengthy, subject to error (and, some might say, corruption), and very expensive. At this very moment there could exist valuable medicine that someone could benefit from but cannot use for many years until the trials are complete.

There are three clinical trial phases in the United States. Phase I assesses the safety of the drug and is relatively quick to complete, taking only a couple of months, as opposed to Phases II and III, which can take many years. Phase II tests the effects of the drug over time and can involve hundreds of people, and Phase III is large-scale testing involving sometimes thousands of people.

A blockchain application can be used to record the results of these trials, and therefore create an immutable record of how the medicine performed. In addition, smart contracts can alert stakeholders of important testing results.

This case is another example where buy-in and cooperation from other agencies will pose a great challenge. Unless the current laws change, it could still take years to approve drugs—even with blockchain technology. However, trust in the data will be higher because blockchain is immutable, and it will be less expensive to record and report on results than the paper-intensive process used today.

STREAMLINING

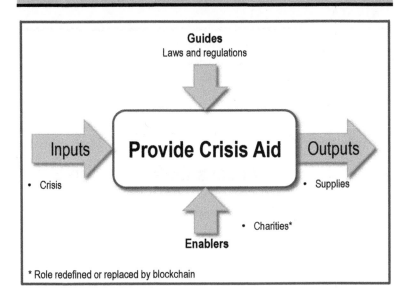

Combined with a crypto-currency such as Bitcoin, funds can be quickly transferred to countries in need, such as in a disease outbreak or natural disaster. A crisis aid blockchain application could allow individuals and organizations to contribute, without the delay caused by intermediaries such as banks. Most citizens in emerging markets have cell phones, and therefore can receive crypto-currency.

There could even be unique currencies created, allowing these coins to be spent only on items deemed appropriate and necessary. For instance, some crypto-coins could be used on food instead of tobacco; this is similar to the existing supplemental nutrition programs of many developed countries.

PRIVACY

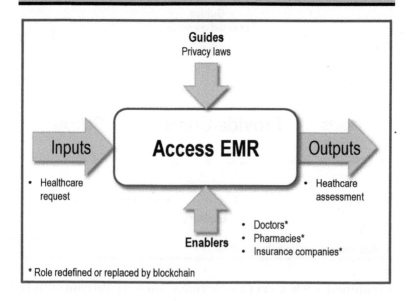

There are many privacy issues involved when healthcare professionals and insurance companies access patient records.

Using the blockchain ledger to store the Electronic Medical Record (EMR) would allow doctors, pharmacies, and insurance companies to access an EMR with permission from the patient. All communication would transpire with public keys and blockchain addresses.

A challenge with this process, however, is to ensure no patient privacy laws are violated such as HIPPA. The patient will need to invoke a smart contract to give medical professionals permission to access his or her EMR.

PERMANENCE

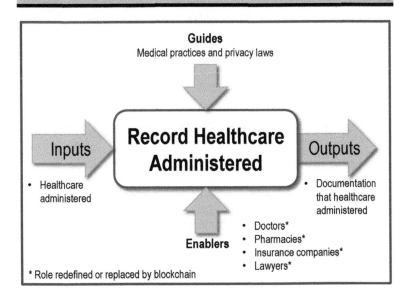

A blockchain application could store records of the healthcare administered to each patient. If there are malpractice lawsuits, then, all of the evidence is immutable and easily retrievable.

This can save legal fees and reduce litigation that is not warranted.

As usual, cooperation of other agencies will prove challenging in this case. Courts will first have to accept such documentation as indisputable evidence. After precedence is established, it will be easier to use healthcare records stored in the blockchain ledger for future cases.

DISTRIBUTION

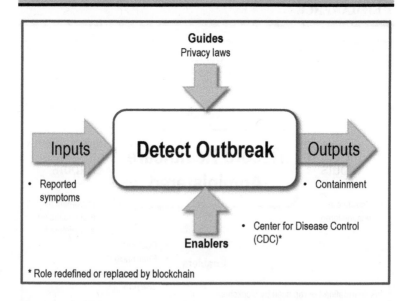

A blockchain application can be used to quickly determine whether a disease is spreading. Medical professionals could record symptoms in the blockchain ledger and the government could quickly react.

Smart contracts could be used to trigger action. For example, an alert could be sent to the Center for Disease Control (CDC) if certain symptoms are being reported in certain areas.

CHAPTER 8

Blockchain within Nonprofit

TRANSPARENCY

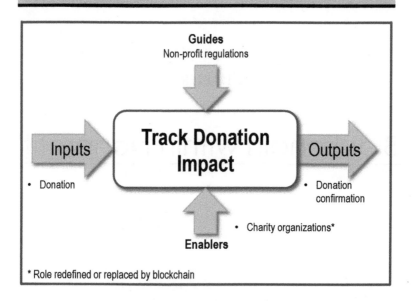

You ever wonder how much of a donation actually goes to the people who need it? Websites like Charity Navigator and Charity Watch rank charities so we can see how much of our donation goes towards the cause, and how much benefits the administration of the charity. Some charity executives earn millions a year in salary.

With blockchain, it is possible to donate directly to an organization, and to track that donation to see how much of it directly helps the cause. Transparency allows a donation to be tracked directly to the recipient.

This not only saves the charity overhead costs, it builds up trust from donors. If a donor sees that 80% of their donation went to the charity organization executives, they will most likely donate to a different charity.

Likewise, an organization will try to reduce administration costs such as executive salaries if they know the donors have complete visibility into the effect of their donations.

STREAMLINING

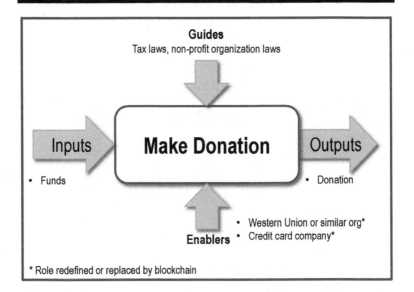

When making a donation, a portion of the donation typically goes to an intermediary to process the transaction, such as Western Union or a credit card company. With blockchain, the donation can go directly to the charity, without using this intermediary.

There is a minimal transaction cost to process a transaction using a blockchain application. As such, more of the donation goes to those who need it. One of the first blockchain applications I have used is Sean's

Outpost, which provides meals to the homeless in Florida (www.seansoutpost.com/).

PRIVACY

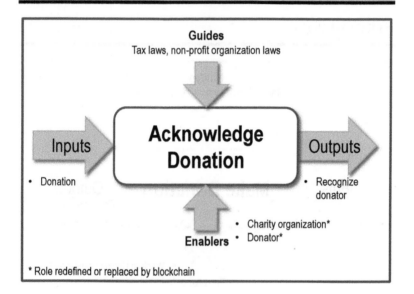

Sometimes a donor does not want to be recognized for their donation. These anonymous donations are easy to make in blockchain using public keys or addresses. The donation can go to those who need it, and the donor does not need to be publicly recognized.

A challenge here, though, is the potential for conflicts of interest that go unchecked with blockchain. For example, a construction company uses blockchain to make a large donation to a campaign fund, with the hope that the politician will favor them with construction contracts.

PERMANENCE

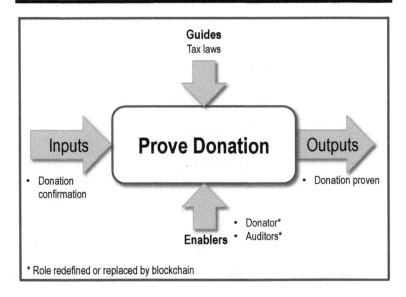

Every year our family accumulates a small stack of paper—letters and receipts from charities acknowledging our donations. Of course, keeping track of all these papers is time-consuming, and keeping such records manually is an error-prone process. It takes space to save the papers, or time to scan each one.

A blockchain ledger can provide an immutable record of the donation. As such, if a donor is audited, he or she can use the blockchain ledger to prove receipt of the donation. Likewise, a tax authority such as the IRS can use the ledger to prove a donation was not made.

DISTRIBUTION

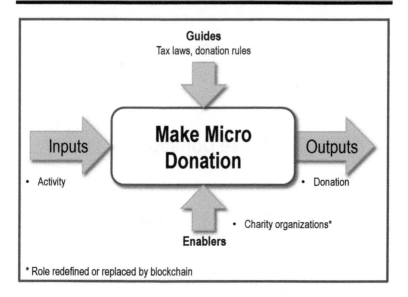

Smart contracts in blockchain can be used to initiate micro-donations to charities. A micro-donation is a very small donation—it could be just pennies or dimes. However, every donation helps; lots of micro-donations can have a substantial impact.

A micro-donation today needs to be made in person with cash, in order to avoid credit card and processing fees, which could reduce the value of a micro-donation to close to zero. The fire service volunteers who wait at traffic lights with buckets for coins are examples of people collecting micro-donations in person.

A blockchain application could make it much easier to make and accept these micro-donations. Smart contracts can be used to initiate micro-donations for events which may not traditionally be associated with a donation, such as:

- An employee quits smoking, and the employer's wellness center made a donation

- For every book that sells, the publisher will donate a quarter to a particular charity

- Whenever the school basketball team wins, parents donate to the Parent Teacher Organization (PTO)

I took a training class on a blockchain technology, and after completing it, a small donation was made by the vendor to a charity of my choice. It was a simple act that made me feel good, and probably boosted the vendor's public image as well.

CHAPTER 9

Blockchain within Media

TRANSPARENCY

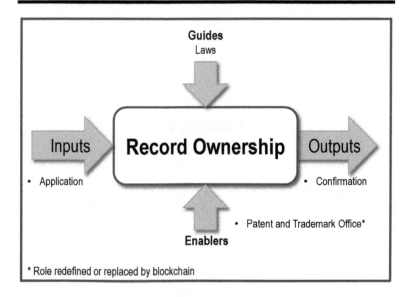

Believe it or not, it is a complex and costly process to record ownership of a song, digital art, or other digital intellectual property. Your ownership must be reviewed with a government intellectual property office.

Blockchain is a natural fit for recording ownership of digital work. A hash can be generated from the work and stored with date information in the immutable ledger. As such, it would be virtually impossible for anyone to contest that they created that work before you did.

There are companies offering this service today using blockchain. Ujo is a blockchain rights database and payment infrastructure. Ujo uses smart contracts to determine the ownership of a creative work.

Even if someone changes a single musical note in a song, it will be treated as a separate song because it will have a different hash, and therefore reduce dubbing and copying.

There is a risk though, that somebody can take someone else's song and change a note or two and record it as their own work, and it would receive a distinct hash code. Someone would need to prove that the newer song was copied from the original. Catching the culprit would be difficult too as all we would know would be their public key.

STREAMLINING

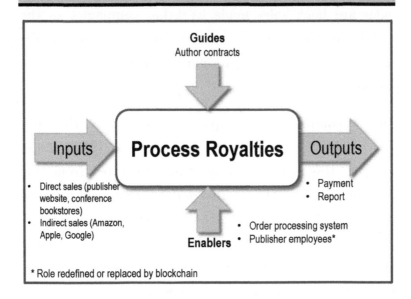

I manage the publishing company Technics Publications. We have published over 100 books, most in the field of data management.

Every six months we pay royalties to our authors. Royalties are payments made to authors which are a percentage of the net sales received. We pay royalties to our authors in July for sales from January through June, and in January for sales from July through December.

We run our royalty reports based on both direct and indirect sources. Direct sales are books that our publishing company sells directly to the public, either through our website or at conference bookstores. Indirect sales are book sales made by other companies to the public, including books sold through Amazon, Apple, and Google. We receive indirect sales reports on a weekly, monthly, or quarterly basis.

In our company, two employees enter all of the sales (both direct and indirect) into our order processing system. Royalty reports are then generated from this system, based on the royalty percentage agreed between author and publisher in the author's book contract. Payment is then made to each author, along with a royalty report. The current royalty process is a very manually-intensive process, taking on average five days per year.

We can introduce blockchain into this process. A blockchain application can free up both employees to spend their time on more productive initiatives. Instead of waiting every week (or longer) for indirect sales reports, as soon as a sale is made on a site like Amazon, a smart contract would notify us of the sale and the author would be paid.

The sale would be recorded in the blockchain ledger and smart contracts would apply the rules of the author agreement to the sale. This would generate a royalty payment to the author in a digital currency such as Bitcoin, or initiate a payment to a traditional bank account or PayPal account.

The author advantages to using blockchain are complete visibility into the entire payment process, and royalty payments almost instantaneously (instead of waiting for up to six months). The publisher saves time and money, too. For example, we would save two employees working five days each to process royalties.

One big hurdle to making all of this work is that the indirect companies have to agree to send us sales data when a sale is made. We can set up payments to our authors using smart contracts, but unless Amazon and others are willing to adopt a similar blockchain process to pay *us*, we could end up paying authors for sales that we have not yet been paid. The entire process would work well if our indirect sellers used smart contracts to instantly pay us when a book sells, and then we could use smart contracts to pay the author moments later.

PRIVACY

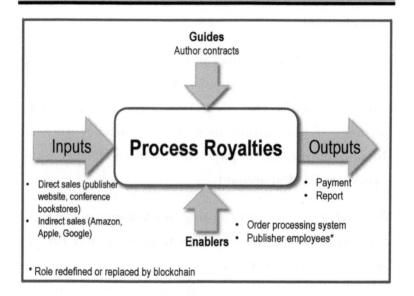

Let's view the same royalties just discussed, but with a different angle. Authors frequently use pen names instead of their actual names. A pen name is used to obscure the *public* identity of an author; it could be used, for instance, if the author doesn't want readers to know whether they're a man or woman. However, no one but the publisher knows the author's real identity.

If the royalties process is performed using blockchain, it's possible for the author to use their pen name even with the publisher, providing more complete anonymity.

For example, if a famous author writes a book outside of their typical genre, and is unsure whether it will be popular, a pen name can protect their identity.

PERMANENCE

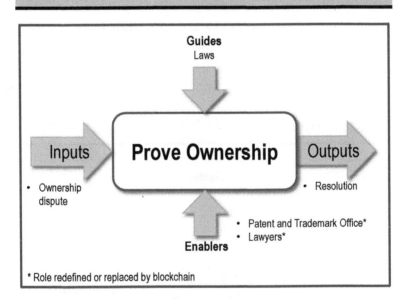

The process of reporting someone for copyright or trademark infringement can take a lot of time and be very expensive.

As we just discussed, a blockchain application can be used to verify proof of ownership—whether it is a song, book, or work of art in question. Once a hash has been created from someone's digital product, and stored in the blockchain ledger, proving ownership becomes easier and less costly.

For example, there is a company called Monegraph that allows artists to record their work in the Monegraph blockchain ledger, and also sell it. Monegraph verifies art ownership.

One obvious challenge, however, is that someone could conceivably record someone *else's* product in the blockchain ledger before the actual author does, thereby assuming ownership; it would be very difficult to prove otherwise.

DISTRIBUTION

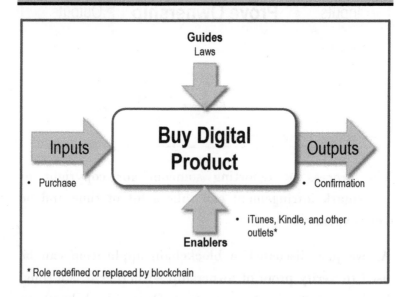

Artists, musicians, and authors can sell their works directly using a blockchain application, circumventing publishers (like our publishing company) completely in the process.

Since you can create new currencies using blockchain, it could theoretically be possible to create a new currency for each musical artist. Fans could buy that artist's "coins," and if the artist becomes more popular, the coins will go up in value.

This is actually happening today with a company called PeerTracks. PeerTracks lets each artist create their own token and choose the quantity of tokens available. Then these can be sold to fans. The value of the tokens is driven by supply and demand.[28]

Singer Imogen Heap and violinist Zoe Keating are currently using blockchain to sell their music, skipping popular intermediaries such as iTunes or Spotify. Imogen explains the concept of a smart contract: "Basically a tiny little program that has fixed instructions about how to move money...you store it permanently on a blockchain, and when payments come in, it says 'we've received some money: this much goes to the taxman, this much goes to our contributor, this much goes to our studio...'"[29]

---

[28] http://bit.ly/2C1Giei.

[29] http://bit.ly/1KSxuaf.

PART III

Blockchain Impact

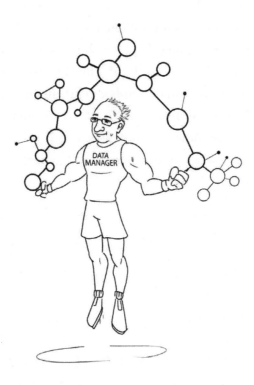

Now that we've explored some hypothetical and real-world case studies on the many applications of blockchain, it's time to turn to the realm of data management. Part III summarizes each of the 11 commonly accepted disciplines within data management, and shows how blockchain will change each one. This often means expanding the responsibilities of those IT and business professionals within each discipline.

The *Data Management Body of Knowledge 2nd Edition* (abbreviated DAMA-DMBOK2) will provide the context and reference for this section. The DAMA-DMBOK2 contains the most comprehensive description of data management in general. This book also provides a fantastic overview of each of the 11 disciplines, plus captures the numerous complex relationships that exist between the disciplines. As such, it's a wonderful tool for examining how new technologies (such as blockchain) will impact data management in general and each discipline in particular.

The DAMA-DMBOK2 visually captures all 11 disciplines in the DAMA Wheel, as shown in Figure III.1.

The DAMA Wheel defines the Data Management Knowledge Areas (sometimes called "domains"). It places data governance at the center of these domains, since governance is required for consistency within and between all of the other functions. The other Knowledge Areas (e.g. Data Architecture, Data Modeling) are equally balanced around the Wheel. They are all necessary parts of a mature data management function, but they may be implemented at different times, depending on the requirements of the organization.[30]

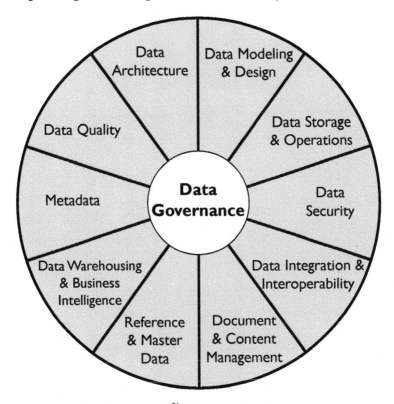

Figure III.1 The DAMA Wheel[31] (© DAMA 2017)

For each of the next 11 chapters, learn about each discipline, and see how roles and responsibilities will change as blockchain becomes more mainstream.

---

[30] Data Management Body of Knowledge, 2nd Edition, DAMA International, Technics Publications, 2017, page 35.

[31] Data Management Body of Knowledge, 2nd Edition, DAMA International, Technics Publications, 2017, page 36.

necessary parts of a mature data management function, but these may be implemented at different times depending on the requirements of the organization.[]

Figure 11.3 The DAMA Wheel[20] (© DAMA 2017)

Job roles of the (next 10) examples learn more new disciplines and new roles and responsibilities will change as blockchain becomes more mainstream.

[] Data Management Body of Knowledge, 2nd Edition. DAMA International. Technics Publications, 2017, page 37.

[] Data Management Body of Knowledge, 2nd Edition. DAMA International. Technics Publications, 2017, page 36.

CHAPTER 10

Data Governance

This chapter provides an overview from DAMA-DMBOK2 on data governance (excerpted from pages 67-74), and then covers the additional data governance responsibilities needed for blockchain to work well within our organizations.

OVERVIEW FROM DAMA-DMBOK2

Data Governance (DG) is defined as the exercise of authority and control (i.e. planning, monitoring, and enforcement) over the management of data assets.

While the driver of data management overall is to ensure that an organization gets value out of its data, Data Governance focuses on how data-related decisions are made and how people and processes are expected to behave in relation to data.

Each organization should adopt a governance model that supports its business strategy and is likely to succeed within its own cultural context. Organizations should also be prepared to evolve that model to meet new challenges. Models differ in organizational structure, level of formality, and approach to decision-making. Some models are centrally organized, while others are distributed.

Data Governance organizations may also have multiple layers to address concerns at different levels within an enterprise—local, divisional, and enterprise-wide. The work of governance is often divided among multiple committees, each with a purpose and level of oversight different from the others.

The following table describes the typical committees that might be established within a data governance operating framework.

Data Governance Body	Description
Data Governance Steering Committee	The primary and highest authority organization for data governance (DG) in an organization. Responsible for oversight, support, and funding of DG activities. Comprises a cross-functional group of senior executives.
Data Governance Council (DGC)	Manages DG initiatives (e.g., development of policies or metrics), issues, and escalations.
Data Governance Office (DGO)	Ongoing focus on enterprise-level data definitions and data management standards across all DAMA-DMBOK Knowledge Areas. Composed of coordinating roles that are labelled as *data stewards* or *custodians*, and *data owners*.
Data Stewardship Teams	Communities of interest focused on one or more specific subject areas or projects, collaborating or consulting with project teams on data definitions and data management standards related to the focus. Consists of business and technical data stewards and data analysts.
Local Data Governance Committee	Large organizations may have divisional or departmental data governance councils working under the auspices of an Enterprise DGC. Smaller organizations should try to avoid such complexity.

ADDITIONAL RESPONSIBILITIES DUE TO BLOCKCHAIN

Data governance increases trust in the data within an organization. In many business processes, the central power authority needs to prove its data can be trusted. Therefore, many central power authorities invest heavily in data governance.

I am not only CEO of my small publishing company which acts as central power authority for many publisher processes, I am also the data steward for author and book metadata. This information must be correct, or I quickly lose credibility from bookstores, distributors, and authors themselves. I am also the data steward for royalty information, and I will quickly lose trust from authors if this information is suspect.

Even if a blockchain application to process royalties is introduced within my publishing company, I still need to act as data steward for royalty information—even though my company is no longer the central power authority. I am still responsible for defining and ensuring the data quality of all of the royalty rules. For example, Bob the author receives 12% royalties. Even though blockchain makes the royalty process quicker and more transparent, I am still ultimately responsible for Bob receiving 12% royalties, and not 8% or 15%.

Blockchain will not replace any activities within data governance. In fact, blockchain adds additional responsibilities to those who work with data governance.

APPLYING DG ACROSS ORGANIZATIONS

DG exists at local, divisional, and organization-wide levels, but what about across organizations or industries? Blockchain applications will make data governance more complex and interesting by crossing organizational boundaries. Your Data Governance Steering Committee may need to meet periodically with the committees from other organizations that are involved in the same blockchain initiative. For example, a group of insurance companies, working cooperatively to build a blockchain application to reduce fraud, would require consistent data governance practices.

In another example, someone buys a book on Amazon, and via a smart contract ten minutes later the author receives a royalty. Do we view terms like "book" consistently? What about the concept of "return?" If the customer returns a book to Amazon, how do we ensure the author's royalty is also returned? Furthermore, from a tax perspective, we must ensure that the publisher and author do not need to treat this particular book sale as generating tax.

When blockchain applications cross organizational boundaries, there will likely exist the need for cross-organization or industry-wide DG committees.

MANAGING PERCEPTION

Does managing data as an asset include managing the perception of the technology used to store that data?

There are a number of applications that have been built using blockchain technology that have a very poor perception among the public.

For example, Silk Road was a website where illegal items could be bought or sold anonymously using bitcoin. The cloak of anonymity granted by blockchain allowed those with poor intentions to conduct business without anyone knowing their identities.

In addition, when we read the news about the latest ransomware attack, payment demands are usually in a digital currency such as bitcoin, which helps to ensure the criminal is not caught.

The Data Governance Steering Committee may need to get involved and possibly work with the marketing department if the perception of blockchain could stand to be improved.

REVIEWING RULES

Smart contracts are used by blockchain applications to enforce rules set out in agreements, standards, and contracts.

How do we know, though, that those rules are actually being applied correctly?

The code written to automate document clauses must be under the review of data governance, to ensure the code is correctly interpreting the rule.

Checking the rules can apply to both business and government organizations. Let's return to our royalty process, for example. Even if the blockchain application successfully transfers royalties to a particular author, if the wrong royalty percent is coded into the smart contract, the wrong amount will be paid to the author, leading to accounting and credibility issues.

Reviewing the rules for data governance also includes making sure that smart contracts (and their interaction with other technologies, such as artificial intelligence or IoT) do not cause ethical issues. For example, imagine a smart contract that uses a number of factors to determine car insurance rates, including Fitbit® sensor readings. The sensor readings can report whether a policyholder had a good night's sleep or not; if a policyholder has a poor night's sleep for several days in a row, their car insurance rates go up, because of their increased risk of falling asleep at the wheel. This insurance hike could be contested by the consumer, crossing the line into ethics and law. As such, data governance may need to get involved and work closely with the legal department.

CHAPTER 11

Data Architecture

This chapter provides an overview from DAMA-DMBOK2 on data architecture (excerpted from pages 97-99), and then covers the additional data architecture responsibilities needed for blockchain to work well within our organizations.

OVERVIEW FROM DAMA-DMBOK2

Architecture refers to the art and science of building things (especially habitable structures) and to the results of the process of building—the buildings themselves. In a more general sense, architecture refers to an organized arrangement of component elements intended to optimize the function, performance, feasibility, cost, and aesthetics of an overall structure or system.

The term *architecture* has been adopted to describe several facets of information systems design. ISO/IEC 42010:2007 *Systems and Software Engineering – Architecture Description* (2011) defines *architecture* as "the fundamental organization of a system, embodied in its components, their relationships to each other and the environment, and the principles governing its design and evolution."

However, depending on context, the word *architecture* can refer to any one of the following:

- A description of the current state of systems

- The components of a set of systems

- The discipline of designing systems (architecture practice)

- The intentional design of a system or a set of systems (future state or proposed architecture)

- The artifacts that describe a system (architecture documentation)

- The team that does the design work (the architects or the architecture team)

Architecture practice is carried out at different levels within an organization (enterprise, domain, project, etc.) and within different areas of focus (infrastructure, application, or data).

The discipline of enterprise architecture encompasses domain architectures, including business, data, application, and technology. Well-managed enterprise architecture practices help organizations understand the current state of their systems, promote desirable change toward future state, enable regulatory compliance, and improve effectiveness. Effective management of data (and the systems in which data is stored and used) is a common goal of architecture disciplines.

Data architecture artifacts include specifications describing existing states, definitions of data requirements, data integration guides, and data assets as put forth in a data strategy. An organization's data architecture is described by an integrated collection of master design documents at different levels of abstraction. These master documents set the standards that govern how data is collected, stored, arranged, used, and removed.

The most detailed data architecture design document is a formal enterprise data model, containing data names, comprehensive data and metadata definitions, conceptual and logical entities and relationships, and business rules.

Data architecture is most valuable when it fully supports the needs of the entire enterprise. Enterprise data architecture enables consistent data standardization and integration across the enterprise.

ADDITIONAL RESPONSIBILITIES DUE TO BLOCKCHAIN

The data architect is responsible for "the fundamental organization of a system, embodied in its components, their relationships to each other and the environment, and the principles governing its design and evolution." Many blockchain applications will expand beyond the environment of the organization, requiring the data architect to think more broadly—even at the industry level, for instance.

REDEFINING "ENTERPRISE"

The biggest challenge facing architects with blockchain applications will be that the term "enterprise" may mean something broader than an organization. The enterprise (also known as *organization-scope*) has traditionally set the limits of the data architect. But now the data architect may be responsible for environments outside the organization. "Enterprise" can mean nearly anything—as broad as an entire industry or ecosystem.

Architects from one company will need to work with architects from other companies to ensure consistent priorities and service level agreements. If we are building a blockchain application for transportation, for example, all organizations involved in the transportation process need to participate in architecture discussions to ensure consistency within the system. If Bill of Lading means something different in one organization than another, this must be resolved (with cooperation from the Data Governance Steering Committee) before building the application.

EMPHASIZING STANDARDS

In the 1990s, many data architects struggled with reporting application definitions. For example:

- What is a data warehouse?

- What is an operational data store?

- What is a datamart?

- How does a staging area differ from an integration area?

These questions are still alive and well in many organizations, yet blockchain introduces new terminology and new architecture. All these additional terms and principles also must be standardized and internalized consistently within an organization.

Even the term "blockchain" can be confusing. Is blockchain the lowest-level tier, which is the chain itself? That is, is it just the ledger? Is it only the protocol? Is it the whole stack? Recall in this book that "blockchain" is defined as the lowest-level tier and "blockchain architecture" refers to the whole stack.

Terms like "bitcoin" are equally jumbled. Coming to consensus on whether bitcoin is a currency or a commodity may take generations.

In addition, there are many standards that need to be defined within any given industry. R3 is currently doing this for finance, Blockchain in Transport Alliance (BiTA) for transportation, and IEEE for IoT. We need more consortiums like these, in more industries, defining more standards.

MAKING MORE DECISIONS

Blockchain demands that the architect make many more decisions. For example, these questions need to be answered:

- Should the application even be developed on the blockchain?

- Is this application going to be a currency, contract, or claim application?

- Is it going to be private or public?

- If private, should it be managed by a single organization or a consortium?

- How many recordkeepers are needed in total?

- How many recordkeepers are needed to make a decision?

It is important to have guidelines so that consistent decisions are made when answering such questions about blockchain.

CHAPTER 12

Data Modeling and Design

This chapter provides an overview from DAMA-DMBOK2 on data modeling and design (excerpted from pages 123-148), and then covers the additional data modeling and design responsibilities needed for blockchain to work well within our organizations.

OVERVIEW FROM DAMA-DMBOK2

Data modeling is the process of discovering, analyzing, and scoping data requirements, and then representing and communicating these data requirements in a precise form called the *data model*.

There are a number of different schemes used to represent data. The six most commonly used schemes are: Relational, Dimensional, Object-Oriented, Fact-Based, Time-Based, and NoSQL. Models of these schemes exist at three levels of detail: conceptual, logical, and physical. Each model contains a set of components. Examples of components are entities, relationships, facts, keys, and attributes. Once a model is built, it needs to be reviewed; once approved, it must be maintained.

The goal of data modeling is to confirm and document understanding of different perspectives. This leads to applications that more closely align with current and future business requirements, and creates a foundation for broad-scoped initiatives such as Master Data Management and data governance programs. Proper data modeling leads to lower support costs and increases reusability opportunities for future initiatives, thereby reducing the costs of building new applications.

A conceptual data model captures the high-level data requirements as a collection of related concepts. It contains only the basic and critical business entities within a given realm and function, with a description of each entity and the relationships between entities.

For example, if we were to create a relational conceptual data model showing the relationship between students and a school, it might look like:

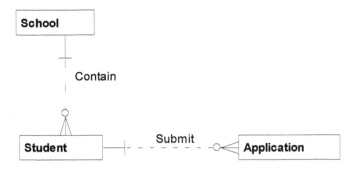

Each **School** may contain one or many **Students**, and each **Student** must come from one **School**. In addition, each **Student** may submit one or many **Applications**, and each **Application** must be submitted by one **Student**.

The relationship lines capture business rules on a relational data model. For example, Bob the student can attend County High School or Queens College, but cannot attend both when applying to this particular university. In addition, an application must be submitted by a single student—not two and not zero.

A logical data model is a detailed representation of data requirements, usually in support of a specific usage context, such as application requirements. Logical data models are still independent of any technology or specific implementation constraints. A logical data model often begins as an extension of a conceptual data model.

In a relational logical data model, the conceptual data model is extended by adding attributes. Attributes are assigned to entities by applying the technique of normalization:

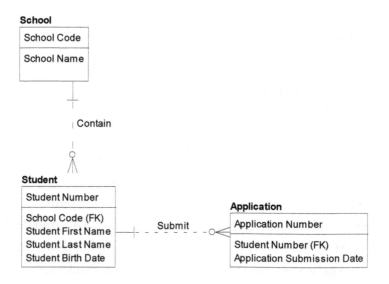

A physical data model (PDM) represents a detailed technical solution. The logical data model is typically used as a starting point, and then adapted to work within a specific set of hardware, software, and network tools. A physical data model is built for a particular technology.

The following figure illustrates a relational physical data model. In this data model, School has been denormalized into the **Student** entity, in order to accommodate a particular technology. Perhaps whenever a Student is accessed, their school information is as well. As such, storing school information with **Student** is a more performant structure than having two separate structures.

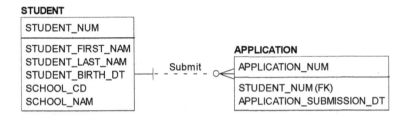

ADDITIONAL RESPONSIBILITIES DUE TO BLOCKCHAIN

"Data modelers are responsible for discovering, analyzing, and scoping data requirements, and then representing and communicating these data requirements in a precise form called the *data model*."

These data requirements can be represented at a conceptual, logical, or physical level. The conceptual and logical levels are independent of technology, but the physical model is dependent on technology. The conceptual and logical therefore, provide insight into requirements and terminology that are true regardless of whether the data is stored in Oracle, Teradata, Hadoop, or in a blockchain ledger. As such, the conceptual and logical models must be built—regardless of how the data will be stored.

MANAGING KEYS

A data modeler is responsible for capturing and documenting candidate keys. A candidate key is an attribute (or a set of attributes) that can be used to identify an entity instance. For example, the candidate key Customer Number can be used to identify customers, such as Bob and Mary.

A candidate key must be unique, stable, and mandatory. Unique means there can never be duplicate values, such as two values of "123" for Student Number. Stable means that once assigned, values can never be updated. Mandatory means we always must have a value. There can never be null or empty values in those attributes that are part of the candidate key.

One of the candidate keys in each entity must be designated as a primary key. The primary key is the candidate key that represents the entity in its relationships with other entities.

Once a one-to-many relationship is drawn from some entity on the *one* side to another entity on the *many* side, the primary key of that entity on the *one* side is copied over as a foreign key to the entity on the *many* side. For instance, Student Number in the Application entity is a foreign key back to Student. This allows us to join tables in a database.

The candidate keys that are not chosen as the primary key are called alternate keys. Primary keys and alternate keys have the same properties of being unique, stable, and mandatory.

We can add alternate keys to our existing logical data model:

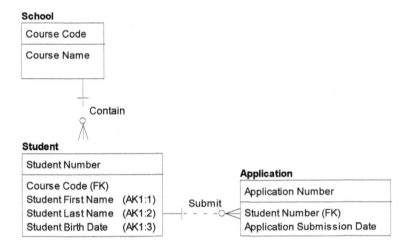

Here we have an alternate key on three attributes: StudentFirstName, StudentLastName, and StudentBirthDate. When there is more than one attribute in a candidate key, it is called a "composite" candidate key. Here we have a composite alternate key on these three attributes.

Returning to the prior physical data model and adding the alternate key, we get this model:

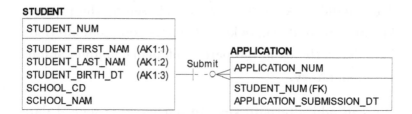

The data modeler must denote the blockchain-specific keys on this model. **STUDENT** and **APPLICATION** will have private keys, public keys, and possibly several blockchain addresses based on public keys.

Each entity will therefore have lots of additional keys for the modeler to manage and denote. In addition, it can be challenging to maintain the mapping between logical and physical data models; all of these additional keys are shown on the physical model only, which will complicate this mapping process.

SKIPPING CONCEPTUAL AND LOGICAL MODELING

Data modelers are often under pressure to deliver a physical data model quickly (and cheaply). Furthermore, project managers and Agile teams rarely see the value of conceptual and logical data models—until it's time to support the application.

This pressure to skip two essential layers of modeling is even more apparent when the underlying database is not relational, like with graph-based or document-based databases.

Blockchain fits under this non-relational type of structure as well. Therefore, the modeler will likely face demand to just design the ledger (and hope that the requirements typically documented at the conceptual and logical levels will magically appear in the physical).

FORWARD AND REVERSE ENGINEERING

It is fairly straightforward to build a relational database design from a physical data model; this process is called "forward engineering." Going from a relational database design to a physical data model, called "reverse engineering," is similarly simple. Often just a few button clicks in our data modeling tools can create a database structure or create a model.

When the database is non-relational, however, it can be difficult or impossible to automate the forward or reverse engineering process. This difficulty is largely due to concepts in a non-relational database that do not have corresponding symbols in our modeling toolkit. For example, nested arrays in document-based databases had no symbol in our data modeling palette until very recently.

Blockchain also introduces new concepts that do not yet exist in our data modeling notations or, therefore, in our data modeling tools. For example, is there a data model symbol to denote a public or private key, similar to notating a primary or alternate key?

Over time, data modelers will need to expand the data modeling toolset once again to automate the processes of building or reverse-engineering a blockchain database.

EMPHASIZING THE LOGICAL

The logical data model is a detailed representation of data requirements, and is independent of any technology. This makes the logical model a very powerful communication tool for everyone involved in blockchain development, because it can be referenced to confirm requirements or business rules.

For example, one of the usages for insurance is to ensure that claims are only paid if the insurance company actually has that policy. These rules are shown on the logical data model. The developer can use these rules and enforce them in the blockchain application, just like in any application. The difference is that the model is not yet forward engineered into blockchain, so the model would be for communication purposes only and not for automatically generating a database structure.

CHAPTER 13

Data Storage and Operations

This chapter provides an overview from DAMA-DMBOK2 on data storage and operations (excerpted from pages 169-180), and then covers the additional data storage and operations responsibilities needed for blockchain to work well within our organizations.

OVERVIEW FROM DAMA-DMBOK2

This domain includes the design, implementation, and support of stored data, to maximize its value throughout its lifecycle, from creation/acquisition to disposal. Data storage and operations comprises two sub-activities:

- **Database support** focuses on activities related to the data lifecycle, from initial implementation of a database environment, through obtaining, backing up, and purging data. Monitoring and tuning are critical to ensuring good database performance.

- **Database technology support** involves defining technical requirements that will meet organizational needs, defining technical architecture, installing and administering technology, and resolving issues related to technology.

Database administrators (DBAs) play key roles in both aspects of data storage and operations. The role of DBA is the most established and most widely-adopted data professional role; database administration practices are perhaps the most mature of all data management practices. DBAs also play dominant roles in data operations and data security.

Companies rely on their information systems to operate. Data Storage and Operations activities are crucial to organizations that rely on data. Business continuity is the primary driver of these activities. If a system becomes unavailable, company operations may be impaired or stopped completely. A reliable data storage infrastructure for IT operations minimizes the risk of disruption.

The CAP Theorem (or Brewer's Theorem) was developed in response to a shift toward more distributed systems (Brewer, 2000). The theorem asserts that a distributed system must make trade-offs between properties, which include:

- **Consistency.** The system must operate as designed and expected at all times.

- **Availability.** The system must be available when requested and must respond to each request.

- **Partition Tolerance.** The system must be able to continue operations during occasions of data loss or partial system failure.

The CAP Theorem states that at most two of the three properties can exist in any shared-data system.

ADDITIONAL RESPONSIBILITIES DUE TO BLOCKCHAIN

The ledger represents the database in blockchain. The DBA will need to align more closely with data architects and data modelers to achieve success with building and supporting blockchain ledgers.

ACHIEVING PERFORMANCE

Recall the CAP Theorem, where you can pick at most two out of three of Consistency, Availability, or Partition Tolerance. With blockchain, however, you can pick all three. We can build a blockchain application that provides a high amount of integrity through multiple recordkeepers, which gives us consistency. The system can always be available and partition tolerant because it is distributed; if a few recordkeepers malfunction, the others will continue to operate.

The cost for achieving all three, however, is performance. Blockchain applications can be very slow because of all of the checking required by recordkeepers. It takes time (and resources) to make sure transactions are accurate, and to make sure that no one is trying to cheat the system.

Performance means the number of transactions that can be processed in a certain amount of time. Bitcoin, for example, currently has a maximum limit of seven transactions per second. Compare this with the VISA credit card processing network, which routinely handles

2,000 transactions per second, and can accommodate peak volumes of 10,000 transactions per second.[32]

The DBA must balance performance with other limiting factors, such as the number of recordkeepers required to confirm a transaction. The more recordkeepers that are used to confirm a transaction, the worse the performance, but the greater the chance that the transaction is valid. The fewer recordkeepers used, the better the performance, but the lower the chance the transaction is valid.

DEFINING PERMANENCE

Blockchain can store the data for "forever." But what does "forever" mean, practically speaking? In some scenarios is "forever" too long?

For example, someone creates their will using blockchain. Fifty years later, someone will have the unfortunate task of invoking that will. Will the smart contract still be there to initiate the necessary transactions?

On the other side, what if an organization needs to delete data after seven years? Can that be programmed into a blockchain smart contract?

The DBA must get involved to make sure smart contracts remain active, and that there is a deactivation or archival process in place for the ledger.

---

[32] http://bit.ly/2mjmFt1.

ACCEPTING MAJORITY RULE

It is very important for mission-critical applications that either the entire transaction completes, or it rolls back. There can be no intermediary state. I can't give $10 to my brother and still have that $10 in my account. It either got transferred to my brother or rolled back into my account.

With blockchain, however, it is not as simple as a "yes" or a "no." "Yes" the transaction completed or "no" it rolled back. Some recordkeepers will say "yes," some will say "no" or not respond, and whether a transaction completes or not depends on a majority vote by the recordkeepers.

The DBA will need to be comfortable in certain scenarios where a majority and not 100% of the recordkeepers confirm a transaction.

SUPPORTING MANY RECORDKEEPERS

The DBA traditionally is responsible for keeping a database server up and running. With blockchain, however, there could be hundreds or thousands of servers that need support. Additional maintenance tools must be created for administration, or additional DBA resources will be needed.

CHAPTER **14**

Data Security

This chapter provides an overview from DAMA-DMBOK2 on data security (excerpted from pages 217-226), and then covers the additional data security responsibilities needed for blockchain to work well within our organizations.

OVERVIEW FROM DAMA-DMBOK2

Data security includes the planning, development, and execution of security policies and procedures to provide proper authentication, authorization, access, and auditing of data and information assets. The specifics of data security (which data needs to be protected, for example) differ between industries and countries. Nevertheless, the goal of data security practices is the same: to protect information assets in alignment with privacy and confidentiality regulations, contractual agreements, and business requirements.

Risk reduction and business growth are the primary drivers of data security activities. Ensuring that an organization's data is secure reduces risk and adds competitive advantage. Security itself is a valuable asset.

Data security risks are associated with regulatory compliance, fiduciary responsibility for the enterprise and stockholders, reputation, and a legal and moral responsibility to protect the private and sensitive information of employees, business partners, and customers. Organizations can be fined for failure to comply with regulations and contractual obligations. A data breach can cost a company the loss of their reputation and their customers' confidence.

As with other aspects of data management, it is best to address data security as an enterprise initiative. Without a coordinated effort, business units will find different solutions to security needs, increasing overall cost while potentially reducing security due to inconsistent protection. Ineffective security architecture or processes can be costly—both through breaches and lost productivity. An operational security strategy that is properly funded, systems-oriented, and consistent across the enterprise will reduce these risks.

A *vulnerability* is a weaknesses or defect in a system that allows it to be successfully attacked and compromised— essentially a hole in an organization's defenses.

Examples of vulnerabilities include network computers with out-of-date security patches, web pages not protected with robust passwords, users not trained to ignore email attachments from unknown senders, or corporate software unprotected against technical commands that will give the attacker control of the system.

A *threat* is a potential offensive action that could be taken against an organization. Threats can be internal or external. They are not always malicious. An uninformed insider can take offensive actions against the organization without even knowing it. Threats may relate to specific vulnerabilities, which then can be prioritized for remediation.

Examples of threats include virus-infected email attachments being sent to the organization, processes that overwhelm network servers and result in an inability to perform business transactions (also called denial-of-service attacks), and exploitation of known vulnerabilities.

Depending on the size of the enterprise, the overall Information Security function may be the primary responsibility of a dedicated Information Security group, usually within the Information Technology (IT) area. Larger enterprises often have a Chief Information Security Officer (CISO) who reports to either the CIO or the CEO. In organizations without dedicated Information Security personnel, responsibility for data security will fall on data managers. In all cases, data managers need to be involved in data security efforts.

In large enterprises, the information security personnel may let specific data governance and user authorization functions be guided by the business managers. Examples include granting user authorizations and data regulatory compliance. Dedicated information security personnel are often most concerned with the technical aspects of information protection, such as combating malicious software and system attacks. However, there is ample room for collaboration during development or an installation project.

ADDITIONAL RESPONSIBILITIES DUE TO BLOCKCHAIN

Data breaches and thefts often make the front page of newspapers and headlines on all media outlets. This sensationalism, combined with increased regulations on protecting data, such as the General Data Protection Regulation (GDPR), make security functions the most visible functions in IT.

Blockchain mitigates security risks in some areas, such as identity theft. It could also expose additional security risks in other areas, such as fraudulent transactions (frequently called "double spends" in blockchain).

COLLABORATING ACROSS ORGANIZATIONS

The first guiding principle of security is collaboration. There are many roles involved within an organization, and these roles must work together to protect the entire organization from security breaches. In blockchain applications, the collaboration most likely will extend outside organizational boundaries and involve IT security administrators, data stewards, audit teams, and legal departments from multiple organizations who will need to work together.

PREVENTING FRAUDULENT TRANSACTIONS

As mentioned earlier, it is possible for an individual or organization to control enough of the recordkeepers to impact consensus of a transaction. For example, if buying a Tesla requires 60% of the recordkeepers to confirm a transaction, and the purchaser controls at least 60% of the recordkeepers, the purchaser can initiate the transaction without paying, have the recordkeepers confirm the transaction was successful, and have the car shipped without payment.

The information security function will need to ensure the system is not compromised. Additional controls will need to be put in place to reduce or eliminate these types of threats.

PROTECTING PRIVATE KEYS

Additionally, the information security function must do what can be done to protect personal and organization private keys.

We often hear about it in the news when mass quantities of credit card numbers or social security numbers are stolen. Imagine someone's private key being stolen. A private key may have access to money, deeds, intellectual properties, accomplishments, and much more. If someone obtains someone else's private key, it would be the most extreme form of identity theft. It would also be anonymous; for certain types of theft, there is very little chance of catching a perpetrator.

In addition to protecting private keys via software, information security professionals may conduct training sessions to educate employees on security concerns with blockchain.

CHAPTER 15

Data Integration and Interoperability

This chapter provides an overview from DAMA-DMBOK2 on data integration and interoperability (excerpted from pages 269-286), and then covers the additional data integration and interoperability responsibilities needed for blockchain to work well within our organizations.

OVERVIEW FROM DAMA-DMBOK2

Data Integration and Interoperability (DII) describes processes related to the movement and consolidation of data within and between data stores, applications, and organizations. Integration consolidates data into consistent forms, either physical or virtual. Data Interoperability is the ability for multiple systems to communicate. DII solutions can enable any number of basic data management functions upon which most organizations depend:

- Data migration and conversion

- Data consolidation into hubs or marts

- Integration of vendor packages into an organization's application portfolio

- Data sharing between applications and across organizations

- Distributing data across data stores and data centers

- Archiving data

- Managing data interfaces

- Obtaining and ingesting external data

- Integrating structured and unstructured data

- Providing operational intelligence and management decision support

The need to manage data movement efficiently is a primary driver for DII. Since most organizations have hundreds or thousands of databases and stores, managing the processes for moving data has become a central responsibility of every information technology organization. Data must be shuttled not only between the data stores within the organization, but even to and from other organizations entirely. If not managed properly, the process of moving data can overwhelm IT resources, and dwarf the support requirements of traditional application and data management areas.

The advent of organizations purchasing applications from software vendors (rather than developing custom applications) has amplified the need for enterprise data integration and interoperability. Each purchased application comes with its own set of Master Data stores, transaction data stores, and reporting data stores; these must integrate with the other data stores in the organization. Even Enterprise Resource Planning (ERP) systems that run the common functions of the organization rarely—if ever—encompass all the data stores in the organization. They, too, have their data integrated with other organizational data.

The need to manage complexity and the costs associated with complexity are reasons to architect data integration from an enterprise perspective. An enterprise design of data integration is demonstrably more efficient and cost-effective than distributed or point-to-point solutions. Developing point-to-point solutions between applications can result in thousands or millions of interfaces, and can quickly overwhelm the capabilities of even the most effective and efficient IT support organizations.

Data Exchange Standards are formal rules for the structure of data elements. ISO (International Standards Organization) has developed data exchange standards, as have many industries. A data exchange specification is a common model used by an organization or data exchange group that standardizes the format in which data will be shared. An exchange pattern defines a structure for data transformations needed by any system or organization exchanging data. Data must be mapped to the exchange specification.

Developing and agreeing on a shared message format is certainly a major undertaking. However, a universal exchange format or data layout between systems can significantly simplify data interoperability in an enterprise, lowering the cost of support and enabling better understanding of the data.

The National Information Exchange Model (NIEM) was developed to exchange documents and transactions across government organizations in the United States. The intention is that the sender and the receiver of information share a common, unambiguous understanding of the meaning of that information. Conformance to NIEM ensures that a basic set of information is universally understood, and carries the same consistent meaning across various communities, thus allowing interoperability.

ADDITIONAL RESPONSIBILITIES DUE TO BLOCKCHAIN

Due to the broad scope of many blockchain applications, and the current dependencies inherent in blockchain applications, DII professionals will need to be closely involved in blockchain development.

MIGRATING TO A DIFFERENT PROTOCOL

DII professionals must work closely with data architects and DBAs in selecting a particular blockchain protocol, and when the time comes, migrating to a different protocol.

If the protocol changes, the amount of work required will be similar to any large migration project. Similar to migrating from DB2 to Oracle or from VSAM to MongoDB, migrating from Bitcoin to Ethereum for example, can lead to complexities—not just with the storage of data but also with application functionality and data access.

MIGRATING TO A DIFFERENT VENDOR PACKAGE

Similar involvement is required of the DII team in migrating from one vendor package to another.

Blockchain vendors might have their own proprietary code and protocols, making it very difficult to migrate to a different platform. In addition to standard protocols, vendors might have their own specific protocols that will not work on another vendor's platform. I have experience with the SAP platform, so I can tell you firsthand of the challenges with migrating to and from the SAP environment.

SHARING DATA ACROSS ORGANIZATIONS

DII professionals must work closely with data modelers and data governance professionals to come up with industry standards for the storage of data in blockchain ledgers.

Since blockchain often crosses organizations, there must exist standards enforced across organizations. Standards (such as NIEM) must be embraced to make blockchain applications that cross organizations successful.

INTEGRATING STRUCTURED AND UNSTRUCTURED DATA

Blockchain, just like any non-relational database, supports both simple (structured) data as well as complex (unstructured) data. The integration problems don't go away with blockchain. We still need to connect unstructured text containing a particular product name to that product hierarchy, or a picture of a customer to the customer ID associated with that customer. DII professionals will need to get involved. There is a greater need for taxonomies, which will be discussed in the next chapter.

CHAPTER 16

Document and Content Management

This chapter provides an overview from DAMA-DMBOK2 on document and content management (excerpted from pages 303-318), and then covers the additional document and content management responsibilities needed for blockchain to work well within our organizations.

Overview from DAMA-DMBOK2

Document and Content Management controls the capture, storage, access, and use of data and information stored outside relational databases. It focuses on maintaining the integrity of and enabling access to documents and other unstructured or semi-structured information. As such, this domain is roughly equivalent to data operations management for relational databases. However, document and content management also involves strategic drivers. In many organizations, unstructured data has a direct relationship to structured data. Management decisions about such content should be applied consistently. In addition, documents and unstructured content are expected to be just as secure and high-quality as other types of data are.

The primary business drivers for document and content management include regulatory compliance, the ability to respond to litigation and e-discovery requests, and business continuity requirements. Good records management can also help organizations become more efficient. Effective management of ontologies and other structures that facilitate searching lead to organized and helpful websites, which improve customer and employee satisfaction.

A document is to content what a bucket is to water: a container. *Content* refers to the data and information inside the file, document, or website. Content is often managed based on the concepts represented by the documents, as well as the type or status of the documents. Content also has a lifecycle. In its completed form, some content becomes a matter of record for an organization. Official records are treated differently from other content.

Content management includes the processes, techniques, and technologies for organizing, categorizing, and structuring information resources, so that they can be stored, published, and reused in multiple ways.

A *controlled vocabulary* is a defined list of explicitly allowed terms used to index, categorize, tag, sort, and retrieve content through browsing and searching. A controlled vocabulary is necessary to systematically organize documents, records, and content.

Taxonomy is an umbrella term referring to any classification or controlled vocabulary. The best-known example of taxonomy is the classification system for all living things developed by the Swedish biologist Linnaeus.

In content management, a *taxonomy* is a naming structure containing a controlled vocabulary, used for outlining topics and enabling navigation and search systems. Taxonomies help reduce ambiguity and control synonyms. A hierarchical taxonomy may contain different types of parent/child relationships useful for both indexers and searchers. Such taxonomies are used to create drill-down type interfaces.

Classification schemes are codes that represent controlled vocabulary. These schemes are often hierarchical, and may have words associated with them. A well-known example is the Dewey Decimal System and the US Library of Congress Classification (which includes main classes and subclasses). As a number-based taxonomy, the Dewey Decimal System is also a multi-lingual expression for subject coding, since numbers can be 'decoded' into any language.

Folksonomies are classification schemes for online content terms and names obtained through social tagging. Individual users and groups use them to annotate and categorize digital content. They typically do not have hierarchical structures or preferred terms. Folksonomies are not usually considered authoritative or applied to document indexing, because experts do not compile them. However, because they directly reflect the vocabulary of users, they offer the potential to enhance information retrieval. Folksonomy terms can be linked to structured controlled vocabularies.

An *ontology* is a type of taxonomy that represents a set of concepts and their relationships within a domain.

Documents are electronic or paper objects that contain instructions for tasks, requirements for how and when to perform functions, and logs of task executions and decisions. Documents can communicate and share information and knowledge. Examples of documents include procedures, protocols, methods, and specifications.

ADDITIONAL RESPONSIBILITIES DUE TO BLOCKCHAIN

Those involved in Document and Content Management will find many opportunities with blockchain as a document storage and retrieval tool. There will be challenges too, though, such as performance.

ENSURING SUFFICIENT PERFORMANCE

Performance is a factor that has come up in many of these blockchain application discussions on additional responsibilities from data management disciplines.

To meet the user's need to store and retrieve documents, blockchain performance must be improved.

As discussed earlier, fewer recordkeepers leads to improved performance. However, this comes with a higher risk of compromising the system; fewer recordkeepers mean less ledger backup.

ENSURING RETENTION AND DISPOSAL

One of the requirements for document management is to dispose of the documents after a certain period of time. Because blockchain is immutable, the documents may never be deleted. Coordination will be required between DBAs and document management experts to deactivate or archive no longer needed documents from the blockchain ledger.

ENSURING INTEGRITY

This chapter has emphasized that document management is responsible for ensuring that an organization's records (and information generated or managed by or for the organization) have a reasonable guarantee of authenticity and reliability. Blockchain can deliver this. Many of the experts in Document and Content Management will become the business users involved in blockchain application development in this area.

ENSURING PROTECTION

This chapter emphasized that document management is responsible for ensuring document protection. The use of public keys can ensure documents and people remain protected. The users in document and content management must work closely with the information security professionals to keep documentation secure.

CHAPTER **17**

Reference and Master Data

This chapter provides an overview from DAMA-DMBOK2 on reference and master data (excerpted from pages 347-352), and then covers the additional reference and master data responsibilities needed for blockchain to work well within our organizations.

OVERVIEW FROM DAMA-DMBOK2

In any organization, certain data is required across business areas, processes, and systems. The organization (and its customers) benefit when this data is shared—when all business units can access the same customer lists, geographic location codes, business unit lists, delivery options, part lists, accounting cost center codes, governmental tax codes, and other relevant data. People using data generally assume a level of consistency exists across the organization... until they see disparate data.

In most organizations, systems and data evolve more organically than data management professionals would like. Particularly in large organizations, various projects and initiatives, mergers and acquisitions, and other business activities result in multiple systems executing essentially the same functions, isolated from each other. These conditions inevitably lead to inconsistencies in data structure and data values between systems. This variability increases costs and risks. Both can be reduced through the management of master data and reference data.

Master data management requires identifying and/or developing a trusted version of truth for each instance of conceptual entities (including product, place, account, person, or organization), and then maintaining the currency of that version. The primary challenge with master data is entity resolution (also called identity management), which is the process of discerning and managing associations between data from different systems and processes. The entity instances represented by master data rows will be represented differently across systems. Master data management works to resolve these differences, in order to consistently identify individual entity instances (specific customers, products, etc.) in different contexts. This process must also be managed over time, so that the identifiers for these master data entity instances remain consistent.

Reference data and master data share conceptually similar purposes. Both provide context critical to the creation and use of transactional data. (Reference data also provides context for master data.) They enable data to be meaningfully understood. Importantly, both are shared resources that should be managed at the enterprise level. Having multiple instances of the same reference data is inefficient, and inevitably leads to inconsistency between them. Inconsistency leads to ambiguity, and ambiguity introduces risk to an organization.

Reference data also has characteristics that distinguish it from other kinds of master data (e.g., enterprise or transactional structure data). It is less volatile. Reference datasets are generally less complex and smaller than transactional or master data sets. They have fewer columns and fewer rows. The challenges of entity resolution do not fall under the scope of reference data management.

ADDITIONAL RESPONSIBILITIES DUE TO BLOCKCHAIN

Those involved with MDM and RDM will find that their work will extend beyond organizational boundaries if blockchain applications are introduced. Many professionals in this discipline might find themselves working with standards organizations to define common master and reference data across their industries.

CREATING CONSISTENT MASTER AND REFERENCE DATA

Master data management and reference data management will most likely cross enterprise boundaries when blockchain is introduced. Organizations will need to cooperate and invest resources to come up with consistent master data and reference data. RDM will have less of an issue than MDM, hopefully, because many of the RDM codes (such as diagnostic or ISO codes) should be industry standards.

MAINTAINING MASTER AND REFERENCE DATA

Even after the initial set of terms is standardized, there must exist a process to keep the data current. If one organization needs to change a reference data value, what process would allow this change to be made? It would need to involve all stakeholders, yet be made quickly so the organization can continue with their business.

Similarly, when standards change, there must be a process in place to update the standards within the application, and to notify all organizations of the change.

Those involved with RDM and MDM will need to work closely with data governance to define the maintenance of these codes in blockchain applications.

RETIRING MASTER AND REFERENCE DATA

When master data and reference data values are no longer needed, what would be the process of removing them from the system? A simple delete can lead to issues with connected data; furthermore, deletes do not occur in the blockchain ledger because it is immutable. There would need to exist a process to "turn off" or deactivate values when they are no longer needed.

Similar to the maintenance activities, those involved with RDM and MDM will need to align with data governance to properly maintain these codes.

CHAPTER 18

Data Warehousing and Business Intelligence

This chapter provides an overview from DAMA-DMBOK2 on data warehousing and business intelligence (excerpted from pages 381-384), and then covers the additional data warehousing and business intelligence responsibilities needed for blockchain to work well within our organizations.

OVERVIEW FROM DAMA-DMBOK2

The concept of the data warehouse emerged in the 1980s as technology enabled organizations to integrate data from a range of sources into a common data model. Integrated data promised to provide insight into operational processes and open up new possibilities for leveraging data to make decisions and create organizational value. As importantly, data warehouses were seen as a means to reduce the proliferation of decision support systems (DSS), most of which drew on the same core enterprise data. The concept of an enterprise warehouse promised a way to reduce data redundancy, improve the consistency of information, and enable an enterprise to use its data to make better decisions.

In the 1990s, we began to build data warehouses in earnest. Since then (and especially with the co-evolution of business intelligence as a primary driver of business decision-making), data warehouses have become "mainstream." Most enterprises have data warehouses; warehousing is the recognized core of enterprise data management.[33] Even though well-established, the data warehouse continues to evolve. As new forms of data are created with increasing velocity, new concepts (like data lakes) are constantly emerging that will influence the future of the data warehouse.

The primary driver for data warehousing is to support operational functions, compliance requirements, and Business Intelligence (BI) activities (though not all BI activities depend on warehouse data). Increasingly, organizations are asked to provide data as evidence that they have complied with regulatory requirements. Because they contain historical data, warehouses are often the means to respond to such requests. Nevertheless, business intelligence support continues to be the primary reason for a warehouse. BI promises insight about the organization, its customers, and its products. An organization that acts on knowledge gained from BI can improve operational efficiency and competitive advantage. As more data has become available at a greater velocity, BI has evolved from retrospective assessment to predictive analytics.

The term *Business Intelligence* (BI) has two meanings. First, it refers to a type of data analysis aimed at understanding organizational activities and opportunities. Results of such analysis are used to improve organizational success. When people say that data holds the key to competitive advantage, they are

---

[33] http://bit.ly/2sVPIYr.

articulating the promise inherent in business intelligence activity: that if an organization asks the right questions of its own data, it can gain insights (about its products, services, and customers) that enable it to make better decisions about how to fulfill its strategic objectives.

Secondly, *business intelligence* refers to a set of technologies that support this kind of data analysis. An evolution of decision support tools, BI tools enable querying, data mining, statistical analysis, reporting, scenario modeling, data visualization, and dashboarding. They are used for everything from budgeting to advanced analytics.

A *Data Warehouse* (DW) is a combination of two primary components: An integrated decision support database and the related software programs used to collect, cleanse, transform, and store data from a variety of operational and external sources. To support historical, analytical, and BI requirements, a data warehouse may also include dependent data marts, which are subset copies of data from the warehouse. In its broadest context, a data warehouse includes any data stores or extracts used to support the delivery of data for BI purposes.

Data Warehousing describes the operational extract, cleansing, transformation, control, and load processes that maintain the data in a data warehouse. The data warehousing process focuses on enabling an integrated and historical business context on operational data by enforcing business rules and maintaining appropriate business data relationships.

ADDITIONAL RESPONSIBILITIES DUE TO BLOCKCHAIN

The data warehouse project team will find additional challenges with extracting data from and loading data to the blockchain ledger.

REMOVING THE HUB

I was a data architect for many years on a data warehouse team, and my daily goal was to do whatever I could do to centralize the data and have one trusted point for reporting.

When thinking about this centralized hub structure, I picture a bicycle wheel:

All data is centralized in one database and all interfaces pass data to or extract data from this hub.

With blockchain, instead of a traditional hub and spoke architecture for applications, we have a completely decentralized architecture. Recall this figure:

If the data warehouse is built using blockchain, the data warehouse project team will need to work closely with data governance to ensure that the data is understood, and its lineage is accurate. In addition, future analytics uses need to be understood and documented.

EXTRACTING (THE "E" IN ETL)

ETL stands for Extract, Transform, and Load; this is the process of extracting data from a source system, transforming it into something useful for business intelligence, and loading it into a data warehouse for reporting. ETL from or to a blockchain application could be complex.

Similar to extracting data from any NoSQL database, developers will need to learn how to parse a ledger and integrate it with the rest of the data in the data warehouse.

An important challenge will be understanding the mapping between private and public keys and ensuring the private key is not stored in the data warehouse (or if it is stored there, it is protected well). Coordination with the security team will be required.

BROADENING SCOPE OF THE DATA WAREHOUSE

A common theme in the challenges across the data management disciplines is the broadening of application scope beyond the organization. For data warehousing and business intelligence, it is extremely challenging to design and report on structures that cross departments and functional boundaries. Blockchain applications can take it a step further, requiring design and reporting across organizations. It is possible to do this, but extremely challenging; it demands heavy reliance on master data and reference data standards.

CHAPTER 19

Metadata Management

This chapter provides an overview from DAMA-DMBOK2 on metadata management (excerpted from pages 417-424), and then covers the additional metadata management responsibilities needed for blockchain to work well within our organizations.

OVERVIEW FROM DAMA-DMBOK2

The most common definition of *metadata*, "data about data," is misleadingly simple. The kind of information that can be classified as metadata is wide-ranging. Metadata includes information about technical and business processes, data rules and constraints, and logical and physical data structures. It describes the data itself (e.g., databases, data elements, data models), the concepts the data represents (e.g., business processes, application systems, software code, technology infrastructure), and the connections (relationships) between the data and concepts.

Metadata helps an organization understand its data, its systems, and its workflows. It enables data quality assessment, and is integral to the management of databases and other applications. It enhances an organization's ability to process, maintain, integrate, secure, audit, and govern other data.

To understand metadata's vital role in data management, imagine a large library, with hundreds of thousands of books and magazines, but no online catalog.

Without a catalog, readers might not even know how to start looking for a specific book or even a specific topic. The catalog not only provides the necessary information (e.g., which books and materials the library owns, and where they are shelved), it also allows patrons to find materials using different starting points (e.g., subject area, author, or title). Without a catalog, finding a specific book would be difficult if not impossible. An organization without metadata is like a library without a card catalog.

Metadata is often categorized into three types: business, technical, and operational.

Business metadata focuses largely on the content and condition of the data and includes details related to data governance. Examples of business metadata include:

- Definitions and descriptions of data sets, tables, and columns
- Business rules, transformation rules, calculations, and derivations
- Data models
- Data quality rules and measurement results
- Schedules by which data is updated

Technical metadata provides information about the technical details of data, the systems that store data, and the processes that move it within and between systems. Examples of technical metadata include:

- Physical database table and column names

- Column properties
- Database object properties
- Access permissions
- Physical data models, including data table names, keys, and indexes

Operational metadata describes details of the processing and accessing of data. For example:

- Logs of job execution for batch programs
- History of extracts and results
- Schedule anomalies
- Results of audit, balance, control measurements
- Error Logs

ADDITIONAL RESPONSIBILITIES DUE TO BLOCKCHAIN

Experts in metadata management must work closely with experts from the other data management disciplines to identify necessary metadata for blockchain applications, and to ensure that this metadata gets captured in the blockchain ledger.

EXTENDING METADATA STANDARDS

Industry standards will become more important (in some cases, critical) for blockchain applications that cross organizational boundaries. In this book, we've mentioned a number of these standards, such as NIEM and BiTA.

Metadata experts will need to work closely with data governance experts to agree on standards (and modify standards where needed) for a particular organization. In addition, metadata experts will need to work with data architects, data modelers, and DBAs to ensure these standards are adhered to in the blockchain protocol and ledger.

In addition, there are meta-standards that underlie these industry standards, such as meta-standards for building smart contracts and achieving recordkeeper consensus. Metadata experts should be involved in open-source collaboratives that focus in this area, such as Hyperledger. Hyperledger is an open-source collaborative effort created to advance cross-industry blockchain technologies. It is a global collaboration, hosted by The Linux Foundation, including leaders in finance, banking, Internet of Things, supply chain, manufacturing, and technology.[34]

REQUIRING ADDITIONAL METADATA

Metadata experts will need to capture additional types of metadata for blockchain applications. They'll also need to raise the importance of certain existing types of metadata, as certain metadata is more relevant to blockchain than others. Here are just a few of the specific types of metadata that are most important in blockchain.

---

[34] https://ibm.co/2r9NGCg.

Business metadata:

- Business rules, specific around smart contracts
- Public keys
- Blockchain addresses

Technical metadata:

- Recordkeeper total count
- Recordkeeper majority needed count
- Hashing and crypto-currency algorithms

Operational metadata:

- Purge criteria, that is when to deactivate data in the blockchain ledger as data cannot be deleted
- SLA requirements, especially around performance
- Archiving rules in the absence of "no deletes"

STORING METADATA USING BLOCKCHAIN

In traditional relational databases, metadata defines the buckets where the data will be stored. An attribute called "Customer Last Name" is the metadata for the actual last name of the customer. However, with non-relational databases like blockchain, the ledger stores text without the requirement of attribute metadata. For example, if only the number "5" is stored in the blockchain ledger, we need metadata to tell us whether this is "5 pounds," "5 dollars," or "5 people."

The metadata experts will need to work closely with data governance and DBAs to ensure proper metadata is stored in the blockchain ledger.

CHAPTER **20**

Data Quality

This chapter provides an overview from DAMA-DMBOK2 on data quality (excerpted from pages 449-452), and then covers the additional data quality responsibilities needed for blockchain to work well within our organizations.

OVERVIEW FROM DAMA-DMBOK2

Effective data management involves a set of complex, interrelated processes that enable an organization to use its data to achieve strategic goals. Data management includes the ability to design data for applications, store and access it securely, share it appropriately, learn from it, and ensure it meets business needs. One assumption underlying assertions about the value of data is that the data itself is reliable and trustworthy (which we describe as being "high-quality").

However, many factors can undermine that assumption by contributing to poor quality data: lack of understanding about the effects of poor quality data on organizational success, bad planning, 'siloed' system design, inconsistent development processes, incomplete documentation, a lack of standards, or a lack of governance. Many organizations fail to define what makes data fit for purpose.

All data management disciplines contribute to the quality of data, and high-quality data that supports the organization should be the goal of all data management disciplines. Because uninformed decisions or actions by anyone who interacts with data can result in poor data quality, producing high-quality data requires cross-functional commitment and coordination. Organizations and teams should be aware of this, and should plan for high-quality data, by executing processes and projects in ways that account for risk related to unexpected or unacceptable conditions in the data.

Because no organization has perfect business processes, perfect technical processes, or perfect data management practices, all organizations experience problems related to the quality of their data. Organizations that formally manage the quality of data have fewer problems than those that leave data quality to chance.

Formal data quality management is similar to continuous quality management for other products. It includes managing data through its lifecycle by setting standards; building quality into the processes that create, transform, and store data; and measuring data against standards.

Managing data to this level usually requires a data quality program team. The data quality program team is responsible for engaging both business and technical data management professionals. They also drive the process of applying quality management techniques to data, to ensure that data is fit for consumption for a variety of purposes. The team will likely be involved with a series of projects, through which they can establish processes and best practices while addressing high-priority data issues.

Because managing the quality of data involves managing the data lifecycle, a data quality program will also have operational responsibilities related to data usage. For example, these responsibilities can include reporting on data quality levels and engaging in the analysis, quantification, and prioritization of data issues.

The team is also responsible for working with those who need data to do their jobs, ensuring that the data meets their needs. The team will also work with those who create, update, or delete data in the course of their jobs, to ensure they are properly handling the data. Data quality depends on all who interact with the data—not just data management professionals.

ADDITIONAL RESPONSIBILITIES DUE TO BLOCKCHAIN

Data quality experts will need to work closely with the data governance team, to clearly determine what data quality will mean in a blockchain environment.

FIXING DATA QUALITY IN IMMUTABLE DATA

Once data is written to a blockchain, it is there forever. So what if the data was written with a mistake? She ordered a coffee without sugar but it came with sugar. He mistyped the product category. He was born in the

22nd century. How do we handle such data quality issues when the data cannot be changed?

Data quality experts must work with data governance to put rules and processes in place to detect and denote a data quality issue, as opposed to having the data quality issue fixed by correcting the data.

REDEFINING DATA QUALITY

The bounds of "data quality" might need to be extended to include attempts to exploit the system. Recall our example of someone buying 100 shares of IBM but tricking the system by not paying for those shares. For those recordkeepers that are misled and store this erroneous information, should this be considered a data quality issue or a security issue, or both?

Just like when fixing any data quality issues, data quality experts will need to work closely with data governance to define rules and guidelines.

Conclusion

Blockchain is a game changer.

A blockchainopoly creates shared responsibility in executing a process, as opposed to the powerful position of a central power authority.

Many buzz words in technology, including blockchain, carry ambiguous definitions. Sometimes the term "blockchain" refers to the actual immutable shared ledger, sometimes to the protocol, sometimes to the application, and sometimes to all three tiers. We define blockchain to be the ledger tier, whereas the blockchain architecture refers to all three tiers of application, protocol, and ledger.

The ledger tier is managed by recordkeepers. The protocol tier provides the language for transaction validation among recordkeepers and the invoking of smart contracts, which are IF-THEN statements. The application tier automates one or more business processes to enhance a user experience.

We can use blockchain applications without divulging private information about ourselves, through the use of public keys and addresses.

A blockchain application supports one or more of these three purposes: Currencies, Contracts, and Claims. Blockchain applications that focus on currency are digital accounting systems—ledgers which record money we send and receive. Contract applications built using blockchain initiate and record transactions by invoking clauses in contracts. Claims applications capture ownership.

There are both public and private blockchains. A public blockchain allows anyone to view the ledger, use the application built on the ledger, and set up computers to act as recordkeepers for the ledger. A private blockchain exists within an organization, and the organization owns the ledger, protocol, and application.

There are three important types of patterns in blockchain: requirements patterns, risk patterns, and process patterns.

Requirements patterns help us better understand usages. There are five requirements patterns: transparency, streamlining, privacy, permanence, and distribution. The reason for building a blockchain application must be for at least one of these requirements patterns. Once we understand these requirements patterns, we can fit them to any industry in order to identify opportunities for usage. We covered over 50 different use cases in this book, crossing many industries: finance, insurance, government, manufacturing, retail, utilities, healthcare, nonprofit, publishing, music, and art.

Risk patterns are general obstacles we may face during blockchain development. Many detailed examples were provided in this book, yet can be generalized into cooperation, incentives, and change patterns. Note that the most challenging obstacles we will face during blockchain application development will be people challenges, such as accepting a new technology, and working together.

Process patterns generalize every process into Inputs, Guides, Enables, and Outputs. Inputs are provided by stakeholders and/or upstream business processes. They may be raw material, data, or any other resource that the process will transform into output. Inputs are transformed by the process into outputs. Outputs are the deliverables and goals of a process. Guides manage and control the transformation of inputs into their planned outputs. An organization's enablers are those reusable resources that are engaged in supporting the process. If the guides are the *rules*, the enablers are the *tools*.

Master these three important types of patterns, and you will know how to best leverage blockchain technology.

The Data Management Body of Knowledge 2nd Edition (abbreviated DAMA-DMBOK2) is a great reference for assessing an emerging technology. We used DAMA-DMBOK2 in this book to explain how blockchain will impact these 11 disciplines: data governance, data architecture, data modeling and design, data storage and operations, data security, data integration and interoperability, document and content management, reference and master data, data warehousing and business intelligence, metadata management, and data quality.

Remember, concepts and principles first, technology second.

As you begin to understand the immense power and potential of blockchain, you'll come to recognize it as a truly disruptive technology—just like the wheel, printing press, computer, web, smartphone, or cloud. And just like these other groundbreaking technologies, once you understand the underlying principles and use them to build a solid foundation, the opportunities are endless!

INDEX

address, 19, 23, 24, 30, 35, 82, 94, 134, 167
Agile, 156
alternate key, 155
application tier, 29
applications
    claims, 34–37
    contract, 32–34
    currency, 31–32
architecture, 142
artificial intelligence, 139
Assembly, 2
asymmetric-key cryptography, 23
attestation, 36
BASIC, 2
BI. See business intelligence
Bill of Lading, 88, 145
BiTA. See Blockchain in Transport Alliance
Bitcoin, 19, 20, 28, 29, 30, 31, 32, 40, 48, 90, 105, 123, 146, 162, 175
bitcoin currency, 29, 138
blockchain
    explanation, 16–19
    how it works, 19–30
    variations, 30–40
blockchain architecture, 19–30
Blockchain in Transport Alliance, 88, 146, 202
blockchainopoly, 11, 212
Brewer's Theorem, 161
Brooklyn Microgrid, 101
business intelligence, 192–97
business process, 50

Byzantine Generals' Problem, 25
candidate key, 154, 155
CAP Theorem, 161
catch to plate, 87
central power authority, 10, 11, 16, 17, 18, 38, 136, 212
CEO. See chief executive officer
Charity Navigator, 112
Charity Watch, 112
chief executive officer, 168
chief information security officer, 168
CIO. See chief information officer
CISO. See chief information security officer
claims adjuster, 69
claims applications, 34–37
classification scheme, 182
Commodore 64, 14
consortium blockchain, 38
content management, 181
content management system, 78
contract applications, 32–34
controlled vocabulary, 181, 182
Create, Read, Update, and Delete, 18
CRUD. See Create, Read, Update, and Delete
cryptograph, 25
currency applications, 31–32
custodian, 135
DAMA Wheel, 130

DAMA-DMBOK2, 7, 130,
134, 142, 150, 160, 166,
172, 180, 186, 192, 200,
206, 214
data administration, 160
data architect, 144, 145, 195
data architecture, 142–47
data governance, 134–39
data governance council, 135
data governance office, 135
data governance steering
committee, 135, 137, 138,
145
data integration and
interoperability, 172–77
data manager, 168
data model, 4, 5, 150, 151,
152, 153, 155, 156, 157,
158, 192
data modeler, 4, 5, 154, 156
data modeling, 4, 5, 44, 150,
157, 158, 214
data owner, 135
data quality, 205–9
data security, 165–70
data steward, 135, 169
data stewardship team, 135
data storage and operations,
160–64
data tier, 28
data warehouse, 145
data warehousing, 192–97,
194
database administrator, 160
database design, 4, 157
database support, 160
database technology support,
160
datamart, 145
DB2, 175

DBA. See database
administrator
De Beers Group, 92, 93
decision support system, 192
Depository Trust Company,
15, 58
Dewey Decimal System, 182
DII. See data integration and
interoperability
Distribution
Adjudicate Claim, 72
Buy Digital Product, 126
Crowdfund, 62
Detect Outbreak, 108
Feed the Grid, 100
Make Micro Donation, 116
Put Money in Meter, 82
Verify Authenticity and
Condition of
Collectibles, 93
document, 181, 183
document and content
management, 180–84
double spend, 169
DSS. See decision support
system
DTC. See Depository Trust
Company
DW. See data warehouse
electronic medical record, 107
EMR. See electronic medical
record
enablers, 52
enterprise architecture, 143
enterprise data model, 144
Ethereum, 28, 34, 175
Filament, 98
Finance
Announce News, 60
Crowdfund, 62
Perform Audit, 56

Report Capital Gain, 61
Settle Trades, 58
Fitbit, 139
folksonomy, 182
Follow My Vote, 79
foreign key, 154
Fortran, 2
forward engineering, 157
function tier, 28, 40, 212
GDPR. See General Data
  Protection Regulation
General Data Protection
  Regulation, 169
Getting the right information
  to the right people at the
  right time, 15
GOTO, 2
Government
  Access Public Records, 77
  Attestation, 76
  Purchase Real Estate, 80
  Put Money in Meter, 82
  Vote, 79
guides, 52
hash, 23, 24, 26, 35, 120, 121,
  125
hashing, 23
Healthcare
  Access EMR, 106
  Detect Outbreak, 108
  Provide Crisis Aid, 105
  Record Clinical Trial
    Outcome, 104
  Record Heathcare
    Administered, 107
HIPPA, 67, 107
Hyperledger, 203
IBM, 15, 39, 58, 60, 61, 209
IEEE, 146
IF-THEN, 2, 28, 33, 40, 212

information technology, 7,
  18, 168
inputs, 51
Insurance
  Adjudicate Claim, 72
  Appeal Claim Decision, 69
  Detect Fraud, 66
  Initiate Claim, 67
  Research Title, 70
Internet of Things, 68, 96, 97,
  99, 139, 146, 203
IoT. See Internet of Things
IT. See information
  technology
iTunes, 15, 127
Koinify, 63
ledger, 16
Lighthouse, 63
Linux, 203
mainframe, 14
Manufacturing and Retail
  Payment, 90
  Transfer Warranty, 89
  Verify Authenticity and
    Condition of
    Collectibles, 93
  Verify Lineage, 86
  Verify Precious Metal and
    Stone, 91
Marine Transport
  International Ltd., 87
Media
  Buy Digital Product, 126
  Process Royalties, 121, 124
  Prove Ownership, 125
  Record Ownership, 120
metadata, 200
metadata management, 200–
  204
Monegraph, 126

National Information
    Exchange Model, 175
NIEM. See National
    Information Exchange
    Model
Nonprofit
    Acknowledge Donation,
        114
    Make Donation, 113
    Make Micro Donation, 116
    Prove Donation, 115
    Track Donation Impact,
        112
NoSQL, 150
ontology, 180, 183
operational data store, 145
operational metadata, 202
Oracle, 153, 175
outputs, 52
Pascal, 2
patterns, 45
    process, 50–53
    requirements, 45–49
    risk, 49–50
PayPal, 19, 90, 123
PC. See personal computer
PeerTracks, 127
Permanence
    Prove Donation, 115
    Prove Ownership, 125
    Purchase Real Estate, 80
    Record Heathcare
        Administered, 107
    Report Capital Gain, 61
    Research Title, 70
    Track Global Climate
        Change, 99
    Verify Precious Metal and
        Stone, 91
permissioned, 37
permissionless, 37

personal computer, 14
predictive analytics, 193
primary key, 154, 155
Privacy
    Access EMR, 106
    Acknowledge Donation,
        114
    Announce News, 60
    Appeal Claim Decision, 69
    Charge Electric Vehicle, 98
    Payment, 90
    Process Royalties, 124
    Vote, 79
private blockchain, 37, 38, 40,
    41, 213
private key, 22, 23, 24, 35,
    157, 170, 197
process patterns, 50–53
Professional Sports
    Authenticator, 94
proof of existence, 76, 77
proof of ownership, 77, 88,
    125
proof of work, 27
protocol, 27, 28, 29, 30, 34,
    37, 41, 146, 175, 203, 213
public blockchain, 37, 41, 213
public key, 22, 23, 24, 36, 121
R3, 146
reference and master data,
    186–89
requirements patterns, 45–49
reverse engineering, 157
Ripple, 28
risk patterns, 49–50
Satoshi Nakamoto, 31
Sean's Outpost, 114
Secure Hash Algorithm, 23
semi-structured, 180
SHA. See Secure Hash
    Algorithm

Silk Road, 138
smart contracts, 33, 34, 40,
     57, 68, 72, 77, 79, 81, 87,
     100, 105, 120, 123, 139,
     163, 203, 204, 212
smart meters, 96
Solar Change, 101
Spotify, 127
Streamlining
     Access Public Records, 77
     Detect Faulty Device, 97
     Initiate Claim, 67
     Make Donation, 113
     Process Royalties, 121
     Provide Crisis Aid, 105
     Settle Trades, 58
     Transfer Warranty, 89
Swarm, 63
T-account, 16
taxonomy, 181
technical metadata, 201
Teradata, 153
Tesla, 169
threats, 167
Transparency
     Attestation, 76
     Choose Energy Provider,
          96
     Detect Fraud, 66

Perform Audit, 56
Record Clinical Trial
     Outcome, 104
Record Ownership, 120
Track Donation Impact,
     112
Verify Lineage, 86
Ujo, 120
unstructured, 173, 176, 177,
     180
US Library of Congress
     Classification, 182
Utilities
     Charge Electric Vehicle, 98
     Choose Energy Provider,
          96
     Detect Faulty Device, 97
     Feed the Grid, 100
     Track Global Climate
          Change, 99
Viant, 87
Virtual Notary, 77
vulnerability, 167
Warranteer, 89
Western Union, 19, 113
WHILE, 2
World Wild Fund for Nature,
     87